Carers and Caring

THE ONE-STOP GUIDE

June Andrews is a dementia specialist adviser and Professor Emeritus in Dementia Studies. She is a Fellow of the Royal College of Nursing, the highest honour awarded to nurses in the UK and in 2016 was awarded the OBE. June advises families, organisations and governments across the world. She is also author of *Care Homes: The One-Stop Guide* and *Dementia: The One-Stop Guide*, which have sold 44,000 copies and feature in an online training programme for family carers and care workers.

Follow her *@profjuneandrews* on Twitter
and *www.juneandrews.net*

Carers and Caring

THE ONE-STOP GUIDE

How to care for older relatives
and friends – with tips for
managing finances and
accessing the right support

June Andrews

SOUVENIR
PRESS

First published in Great Britain in 2022 by
Souvenir Press,
an imprint of Profile Books Ltd
29 Cloth Fair
London
ECIA 7JQ
www.souvenirpress.co.uk

10 9 8 7 6 5 4 3 2 1

Typeset in Dante by MacGuru Ltd
Printed and bound in Great Britain by
CPI Group (UK) Ltd, Croydon, CR0 4YY

A CIP catalogue record for this book is available from the British Library.

ISBN 978 1 80081 000 6
eISBN 978 1 78283 960 6

MIX
Paper from
responsible sources
FSC
www.fsc.org
FSC® C171272

Dedicated to Sonia Mangan, who has taught me
so much about caring and being a carer, and that
you must allow yourself to be cared about.

Contents

Introduction

Who is a carer?

To those people who have a relative or friend that they care for, it might seem odd that this is even a question. It needs to be asked for two reasons. First, because sometimes the people who are paid to care for another person as part of their job are also sometimes called 'carers'. And second, because family and friends who do caring work often say that they are not 'carers'. The position is very different between, on the one hand, those who work with older people as their job and, on the other hand, family and friends who are caring for someone. Sometimes also known as 'informal carers' or 'unpaid carers' or even 'family carers', the carers in focus in this book are people who provide care as an act of love, loyalty, duty, kindness – or even by accident – looking after an ill, older or disabled family member, friend, partner or someone in their community. It may be a few hours a week or round the clock every day, in their own home or from a distance. It may be temporary or for the rest of the life of the carer, or the person cared for. To make things as clear as possible in these pages I will always talk about nurses, social workers, home helps, care assistants and other people who care for their living as 'care workers'. Only friends, neighbours, family and partners will be described as 'carers' throughout this book.

You may be a family member or friend who rejects the idea of being called a 'carer'.

I am NOT her carer. I am her HUSBAND. (Older man at a carers' support meeting)

Having been her husband for forty years, this man doesn't like anyone coming along and defining their relationship and labelling the ordinary acts of his daily life as 'care'. Anyone can understand why he objects to being branded like this. But here is a signal – throughout this book you will see advantages of allowing others to call you 'a carer'. Because what others say doesn't change your relationship, you may as well allow them to use this label. This is because a lot of the outside help that is on offer is only available to anyone defined as a carer. Obvious examples are when health and social services talk about 'Carer's Allowance' and 'carer's rights'. The language used in their regulations, laws and administration is an imposition, but it is vital to you and to the one you are caring for to take any help that is labelled in this way. It opens the door to a range of rights and possible benefits. Anything you can do to maintain your fundamental role and position as husband, daughter, wife, son, friend, neighbour or relative is important to you and the person you care for, but if you allow yourself to be known in addition as their 'carer', it just makes your life easier. No one likes being put in a box, but there is a good reason to be pragmatic about this definition.

About this book

Who needs this book? Carers, as defined. The aim is to save you time and reduce the cost of caring by advising on common problems and ways round the system, and sources of help. Carers need practical advice that is easy to read and based on experience and evidence. Some official processes are complicated and look like they were devised and written by a person who has never actually had to care. It can take time to search for answers, being referred from pillar to post, when dealing with health and social care processes.

The focus here is on those carers who are caring for older, frailer people. Many of the problems are similar for people who care for younger people, people with complex health needs or children, but there are very important differences which are not the main subject of this book and cannot be covered here. However, the Useful Contacts and Resources section contains links to resources for carers on a range of conditions that impact throughout life, and these also highlight resources that might help parents and others who are carers for children and young people.

Caring can be a joy and a privilege. It's part of human life to care for others, and for many people the involvement is a source of great happiness. Being close to the person you care for, expressing love and making them comfortable and happy is a wonderful experience. Especially in old age and towards the end of life it is a chance to give back to people who have given of themselves all their lives. If you are having such a wonderful experience, some of the things in this book will seem antagonistic. This is because the book is about helping, and the focus is on where things have gone wrong, are difficult, or could be made better. This is not to suggest that caring is always tough. The 'Joy of Caring' is maybe the next book for me to write. Highlighting and offering solutions to the tough stuff is intended to make your caring experience less difficult now, allowing more space for the joyful stuff.

A lot of the time, when you are a family or friendship carer, some aspects of life will not have changed from how it was before you were caring. You are living with or caring for the same person that you have always known. You know the sort of thing that makes them happy and relaxed. You have a shared history. You also know what will upset them and even set them off on a negative way of thinking or responding. You are the expert on this person and how they live. But even an expert needs some fresh ideas occasionally.

The population of carers is not static, so the number of people who might benefit from a book like this is greater than the number of carers at any point in time. It's clear that more than half of us will become a carer at some stage. So, if it has not started for you yet, you have time to prepare by thinking about it now, both from the point of view that you might be a carer but also that one day you might need to get someone to care for you or help you find an alternative such as residential care.

I tease my mother when she is telling me off. I say, 'Be nice to me because I'll be choosing your nursing home.' She laughs, but I'm not exactly joking. (C, 23)

In many countries, children legally must either pay for care or otherwise provide care for their frail older parents. It is not an optional kindness that is done by fond children for their revered elders. It's just a law, even if you are estranged from your parent. You can read more about family dynamics in Chapter Four.

There is already a trend of demanding resources from adult children in the UK, over and above what we willingly give or do for our elderly parents. Normally people in need of care must use their own cash or sell any property they own to pay for it. When they run out of resources, the state will pick up the bill. But if they have previously made gifts to their own children in advance of needing this care, the local authority, unsurprisingly, will claw back significant amounts of that cash or property from the children. If your parent gives you a substantial gift, it is not really your property until it is clear that your parent won't be dependent on state-funded care. You need to be ready to hand it back, so don't spend it.

My dad gave me this money five years ago to help me start my business. Now the council want it back. I'm effectively being charged for my parent's care! (Son)

There is a whole chapter on finance in Chapter Three. Families are often involved in topping up care home fees, over what the local authority gives, if the preferred local care home costs more than the state is prepared to pay. This often happens if the parent has no resources and is getting care paid by the local authority. It is meant to be a voluntary contribution and for luxurious extras, but in some places the difference between the council rate and the local care home charge is significant, so topping up by the family is more or less required.

At the time of writing, in early 2022, the world is still reeling from the COVID-19 pandemic. This tragedy, which started to unfold in late 2019, has seen a disproportionate number of deaths in older people, including devastation of care home resident populations and deaths in hospital. The long-term impact on the health of the population can only be imagined at present. The long-term impact on economics and public deficits is already obvious. Life was very hard for older people during the pandemic, confined to their homes and often not allowed any visitors. When they were eventually allowed to go out many were still too afraid to, having lost their confidence, and in some cases their skills. Depression was common and cognitive decline increased.

The pandemic has hit the fast-forward button on ageing for millions of older people. (Caroline Abrahams, Director, Age UK)

The increased burden of caring remotely and worry about the older people in families and communities had a significant cost for carers. Social services and the NHS rely on carers. Most of us will need help at some point, especially as we ourselves reach later middle age. The pandemic has increased this need at the same time as causing financial and health difficulties for people who have caring responsibilities. This book aims to help you with this.

In other books that I have written, readers have noted that I repeat some information in more than one chapter. That is to make it easier to use the book.

You will find sections that are dedicated to big subjects like money, family relationships and your health. Further on there is a big alphabetical list of practical advice in Chapter 7. You might not need all the advice at the same time, so an A to Z should help for anyone who is just dipping in. Right at the end is a list of key organisations in Useful Contacts and Resources, where you will get more information when you need it.

You can read this book from end to end, but if you only want to find out about one issue that is currently relevant for you, repetition of key information saves you from the effort of checking back and forth with a lot of cross-referencing. If you are a carer, time is short for you, and I don't want to take up more time than is necessary. Some key terms and organisations are given in **bold** to help you do further online research if you wish. It is hoped that the information, sources of help, and experience shared in this book will give you a gift of time, to more than repay any time you spend reading it. I know that this book can only scratch the surface for some people, but it should act as a signpost and encouragement, focused in one volume, when your time and energy are in short supply.

One last important point is this. There are two readers to

address here. One is anyone who is caring now. The other reader to address is anyone who might one day be cared for. And that could be any of us. Maybe you should be thinking now and talking to family and friends about how care will be organised for yourself, however far into the future. Anyone who knows what it is like being a carer will surely want to make life easier for those who might in turn have to organise or provide care for them in the future. You know from experience how hard it is, and a key message is that we all need to plan ahead.

Chapter 1

What sort of person becomes a carer?

This book is not about me, though I am a carer too. How many carers there are depends on the way they are counted, but we are numbered in millions, including those who do not think of themselves as carers. Carers UK, a charity that supports carers, said in 2019 that one in eight adults (around 6.5 million people) were carers in the UK. Women have a 50:50 chance of providing care by the time they are 59; men by the time they are 75. This reflects the fact that currently, working-age women are likely to have caring responsibilities in addition to work and family obligations. Men are more likely to become carers after retiring from employment. The 'young old' are caring for the 'old old' in many cases. At 75 a man may be driving his mother to the shops, doing her garden and cooking for her. A 70-year-old woman may already have been doing this for years for her father who is entering his nineties. If he lives to be 100, as many of us will, she'll be his carer in her eighties. If she doesn't look after herself, she may even die before him. Either way, it is a far cry from what many people think of as 'retirement'. And then there are the huge numbers of children and young people who are balancing caring with trying to get on with school or college. This chapter explores some different kinds of carers.

Sometimes people wake up and discover that they have become a carer without even noticing. It starts with a little bit of help with the shopping, and doing a bit of paperwork now and again, and the next thing you know, you are cooking, doing cleaning and changing beds. Or it starts with you having to respond to occasional comments from a neighbour, and odd phone calls at night or when you are at work. Or a call from the police. After that you may find yourself having to deal with issues every day and night of the week. There is no job interview. The job just happens to you. There may be others who are equally qualified to do it, such as other family members, but they just transpire not to be around or believe they don't have the necessary skills, so you are appointed. And, unlike any other employer the person you are working for may spend a lot of their own energy draining your energy by telling you to go away, and to stop what you are doing. That makes it even more exhausting. You not only have to do the work but argue about it or find a way of doing it covertly. Even more difficult, if you call in some extra help for yourself and them, such as a social work service or a nice local cleaner or gardener, the person you are trying to support may send them away and refuse to accept them. They say they don't need help, and then you as the carer end up having to provide it anyway.

I couldn't bear it. The neighbours could see the state his house was in. I felt it reflected badly on me, and so I used to go in and clean as much as I could until he would tell me to 'beat it'. I did my best. He wouldn't allow a cleaner. I did get one but he 'sacked' her. (Daughter, 70, of Graham, 96)

When we provide care, it is not always from a sense of emotional or moral responsibility. It might be more a matter of circumstance and practicality. People may choose to do required care themselves as much as possible, to reduce the financial cost to the whole family and conserve the family resources, or it might be that the system is too puzzling to navigate.

There is too much paperwork for me to deal with. No matter what I do to try to get into the system, it's like this is a club that I can't get membership of. (Carer)

In some languages there is no word for a 'carer'. The concept doesn't exist for those people who look out for older people in that culture. The things that 'carers' do for their older friends, neighbours and family are just part of normal living and not noticed or described in their language. It didn't have the current meaning in the English language in the past. Why do we now need the word? The answer is mainly because the level of care that must be provided is so much greater every year, and it has a significant impact on the physical, mental and economic well-being of the people doing the caring. Why has that changed? The numbers of people living into greater old age have increased radically, and the numbers of older people living with chronic health conditions have also increased. Older people are older. Poorly people are more poorly. And so, many people are living with even greater age-related impairments. Also, significantly, the wider responsibilities of people who might become carers have increased, as more women have become active in the workplace and their children are dependent for longer.

My dad was out at work by the time he was 14, and in the army doing his National Service at 18, abroad, and came back home married with a child at 21. At 23 my twins are still in full-time education and being looked after by me at home. And I look after Dad as well. (Mary, daughter of Dan, 93)

Mary has a full-time job, cares for her father and still supports her children in their twenties. This is modern life.

Carers of older people can be family or friends. They may be older, or younger, in some cases considerably younger, than the person they are caring for. They may be nearby or a long distance away. It has been said in this book that more than half of family carers are female relatives, but any of us will be a carer at some point in our lives. It can happen because you are 'that sort of person', but it also happens to people who would not see it as part of their nature. Research in 2020 done by Carers UK demonstrated that every day another 6,000 people take on a caring responsibility. That is over 2 million people each year in the UK. About 25 per cent of carers have a disability themselves.

That same report outlined that almost 40 per cent of carers are struggling to make ends meet. Many use their own income regularly to pay for care or support services, equipment or products for the person they care for. Carers, clearly, do not save for their retirement. There is more about finance in Chapter Three.

According to the NHS website it takes carers an average of two years to acknowledge their role. For a long time, things go along with changes so small you don't notice, and then one day you take stock and realise that a significant percentage of your waking life is being spent putting someone else's needs before your own. Sometimes it is a crisis in your own circumstances or health that brings it to your attention.

I had been feeling unwell from time to time but just put it down to my age. Then one day I had some symptoms that had me call the doctor and it turned out I had to go into hospital quickly. My first thought was how was my mother going to survive. Who was going to take her food in? Did I have time to fill up her freezer and arrange for someone to go round and heat a meal up for her? When I spoke about this to the nurse in the emergency room she said, 'As you are a carer, here is the number of an organisation that might be able to help.' It never crossed my mind before then that this is what I am. (Morika, daughter of Emrie, 86)

As with Morika, it sometimes just happens. It goes on for so long that you just see it as part of normal life. This is because it is hard to separate the caring role from the relationship you already have. It may even be that you have become ill and the illness you have has been made worse by caring. You have been burning the candle at both ends, by trying to do everything for someone else as well as living your own life. It doesn't always start because you are planning to take over someone's needs and prioritise them.

I go to see my dad because I just want to see my dad. I'd miss him. He's so kind and funny. Over time, it has started that when I get there I notice little jobs that he hasn't done, and I just end up doing them for him. I didn't regard myself as a carer. But when the pandemic lockdown started and it was said I couldn't go to his house, I realised he'd be in a pickle, so I registered myself as his 'carer' and that meant the new rules allowed me to come and go. Because he really needed me by then. (Dolores, daughter)

Particularly if you are very young, others may not realise you are a carer. A young person might not tell other relatives, friends, schoolteachers or health and care professionals about the responsibilities that they have taken on. They may be afraid of being separated from those they are caring for.

After Dad died, Mum just went AWOL. I was doing all right with my brother, making sure that he was fed and washed and going to school. I realised the social work might come and split us up. He'd already lost him and her and I didn't want him to lose me as well. So I told no one and told him to lie about Mum but I got caught stealing. (Agnes, 15)

Despite her best efforts, Agnes got found out, and the system swung into action. In this case a good outcome was achieved because a foster placement was found for her and her brother, to keep them together, keep him in school and allow her to start an apprenticeship. Many young carers are like Agnes, caring for siblings, but sometimes they are closely involved in the care of older or very old relatives.

On the days when Mum is on a late shift at the hospital I go round to Grandad's after school and make his tea and get him ready for bed. I do my homework there until Mum gets back at about nine. (Ellis, 14)

The anxiety about social workers moving in and taking over which was felt by Agnes is also experienced by older carers. Even when told about benefits that might come from contact with the social work service of the local authority, an older person might not want to involve them.

I don't want them round here asking their questions and prying into my business. They'll be telling me that Arnold has to go in a home, and I'd never see him again. I'm managing fine and they can just stay away. (Mavis, 89, wife of Arnold, 92)

Although more than half of us will have a caring role at some point in our lives, it is more likely for women. The responsibilities that you carry then may need to be juggled with other responsibilities, such as a job. And you may be caring both for an older generation and a younger generation at the same time, because you care for grandparents or parents while still supporting children.

The sort of person who becomes a carer and the responsibilities that a carer undertakes are so wide-ranging that it is hard to cover all of these in one book. You may know a young person like Ellis who is a carer, but you do not identify them as such. Every carer is different, but in this chapter we look at some of the different sorts of people who become carers, with challenges of their own in being identified and in accessing care and support from professionals. This includes young carers, very old carers,

carers from specific ethnic communities, carers from the LGBT+ community and remote carers.

Becoming a carer

Everyone responds to the challenges of caring in different ways. I am in awe of the carers I meet and how they manage. Becoming a carer can feel as if you have lost something major. You have lost some freedoms and you may be mourning the loss of health and well-being of the older person you are caring for. Here are some of the common feelings people have when discovering that they are a carer.

Denial is when you do not let yourself see what is happening. You notice change but you don't accept it for what it is. Not everyone wants to talk or even think about it when they find that they are needing to care for someone, perhaps a person who has a terminal illness or who has become frail, and not the strong person they used to be. It can take time to find ways of coping with that reality, and there will be moments when you don't want to accept what is happening. It's not unusual to feel like this. It is a coping mechanism that gives you time to adjust, but you can't stay like that forever. Just as you are reading this book, at some point every carer must start looking at the practical implications of what is happening and get the information that is needed to work out a plan. But that doesn't happen in the first stage.

Anger is understandable. Your frustration and concern about how unfair this is may build up so much that you want to express it, but you need to find a place where it is safe to do so. In the heat of the moment it is possible to say things that you will later regret. You may have worked hard all your life and be on the threshold of a well-earned leisurely retirement, which now looks like being stolen. Of course you are angry. You may be exhausted with the demands of work and your children, and now in addition an older relative needs your time and attention. Not expressing that anger but bottling it up causes stress. At this time, you need to talk to someone. Anger can make you unwell.

Grief may arise from the sorrow you feel for what the other person is losing, and what you are losing yourself. The need to care for one parent may coincide with the death of another. Instead of taking rest and distraction from your grief you may find yourself busier than ever. You may be caring for someone who constantly mourns the parent that you have lost, and seeks your support and sympathy at a time when you need support and sympathy for yourself. Don't undervalue yourself and the wonderful work you are doing as a carer. Take consolation from your religion or faith. Take comfort from friends and family. You are allowed to grieve.

Stress is the reaction of your body to pressure. Research has shown that the three major causes of stress are poor health, money and work. You will probably experience pressure in all three of these areas as a carer. Caring often adversely affects the health of the carer. It causes additional unexpected and sometimes unmeasured financial burdens, and it creates work pressures that will interfere with the other work in your life, whether that is employment or your other family or social obligations. Juggling all those responsibilities creates stress. So, three major causes of stress are on your plate, not counting other issues that will emerge from time to time. Stress is greater when there are things that you can't control. The advice given often to reduce stress is to 'let go', but there is so much here that you cannot let go of. Hopefully some of the information in this book, or the organisations mentioned here, will be helpful in reducing some of the stresses so that you can scrape together some time to relax. Who knew that twenty minutes to close your eyes and listen to music, or meditate, or pray would be such a rare gift?

Resilience is the ability to recover from setbacks. You still feel the anger, grief and pain, but you are able to keep functioning. To do this you need to take care of yourself and not be afraid to ask others to help take care of you. Your resilience may be knocked, but you can recover. Remember that friends are not a luxury; they are a necessity for maintaining your health and sanity. You need friends for you to be happy and you may need to tell them overtly that you need them. If you give them specific jobs to do for you it will help them know what you need from them.

In those languages where there is not even a word for 'carer', caring for someone when they are sick and vulnerable is simply what you do. We use the word in English because our system needs to identify the people who are doing the work of caring. There are 'Carer's Allowance' and 'carer's assessments' and 'carer support groups'. You can't access any of these unless you are identified as a carer. Organisations like Carers Trust and their partner organisations around the UK are there to help you with advice on caring ... but also with companionship at what can be a lonely time. Their details are at the end of this book. In Scotland there is a website called Care Information, and NHS Choices in England has a wealth of wide-ranging information for carers on its website. This includes advice on getting time off work, types of carer breaks, how to take care of yourself, managing relationships and other issues, including hints for male carers who sometimes face practical problems because our society in general unfairly expects carers to be female. This advice is backed up by tools to assess your physical fitness and mental well-being. They take only moments to use and are connected to good advice about staying well. You must look after yourself if you are going to be able to help others.

Young carers

The term 'young carer' is often used to describe a person between 5 and 18 years old. People aged 16 to 25 who are carers are referred to as a 'young adult carer'. All young people are probably expected to do some jobs around the home, but 'caring' involves doing extra cooking and cleaning or helping someone to get dressed or move around. It includes emotional as well as physical support. There is advice for young carers in the Big List in Chapter Seven. The responsibility for caring should not be on young shoulders. Young carers need to know that others have responsibilities as well, including social services and adult family and friends.

Older or very old carers

The number of carers aged 85 and over in the UK grew by almost 130 per cent in the decade from 2005 to 2015. According to Carers UK and Age UK this group is often invisible, with many older carers providing long hours of vital care and support as their own health and well-being deteriorates. When that was published the number of carers in that age group was predicted to double again by 2035. We need to be reminding those younger than ourselves that this is coming down the line for them and there may be benefits from making plans early. Nearly half of carers age 75 and over are caring for someone with dementia.

Interviews conducted on behalf of the organisation Independent Age revealed that the responsibilities of caring can dominate an older person's life, placing a strain on their physical and mental health. Typically, those they interviewed were caring for a partner with age-related illness or disability, the sort of conditions described in Chapter Two of this book. Some of them were not claiming the Pension Credit, Carer's Allowance and Attendance Allowance that they were entitled to. (There is more information about these allowances in Chapter Three.) The numbers reflect that the older carers were more often than not living with the person they cared for. They may have had support from other family members, but still they felt they could not leave the house for long because of anxiety about their dependent relative. Even though caring is done from love, the research showed that the relationship can be emotionally complex and even fraught.

I do not mind caring for him, but I don't like him very much. The dementia has changed his personality. It's like living with a stranger. (Wife about her husband, 92)

Of the older carers, some are people who have been carers for most of their working life, perhaps with a child who was born with a disability, and they have grown old while caring.

My son Gerald has Down's Syndrome and we've had a lovely life together but now he is 55 and has dementia, so he is like a wee old man. I'm only glad I'm still here to see him through this, now his mother is gone. (Arthur, 78, widower, father of Gerald)

For others the caring responsibility began more recently. Particularly for those over the age of 85, there needs to be a greater focus on promoting the well-being of the carer themselves. They will be subject to the same age-related changes described in Chapter Two. There is plenty of advice available about the right to social work assessments, and for eligible needs to be met including the provision of advice and assistance to access the support that is available to them. The real challenge is in getting hold of that support. Health and social care workers and departments struggle to find ways of implementing the strategies that already exist. It is the eternal problem of making things happen.

Many older people are reluctant to accept care. More work needs to be done to make them feel better able to reach out for it. Focusing on what keeps older carers well will help delay the day when outside care is needed. This makes financial sense, and supports the wish that people have to keep a private family relationship with their loved ones at home for as long as possible.

If you are an older carer, you will find sources of help from Age UK, Carers UK, Carers Trust and other similar organisations listed at the end of this book and throughout other chapters. These voluntary organisations have knowledge and understanding of what you are going through and won't tell you what to do but can open windows as to what is possible. I won't say "open doors", because sometimes you can see what you want, but maybe still can't get it.

Specific ethnic carers

We have found at the Wai Yin Society that older Chinese carers need more support. Although many find caring a rewarding and loving expression of their relationship with the care recipient, they also tell us that they feel invisible and undervalued. (Independent Age Blog)

In the UK there are health inequalities within different white populations and also between different specific ethnic minorities. The picture is complicated, and we do not understand it very well because not enough research has been done in this area. For example, we know that people from Traveller, Bangladeshi and Pakistani communities have the worst health outcomes across a range of indicators. It is suggested that living in crowded accommodation and having mainly low-paid work is a significant factor, but there are many other aspects to consider, such as access to education, language difficulties, systematic prejudice and problems with the attitudes of some of those who are employed to help.

Older carers from specific ethnic communities may have difficulty in accessing advice and information in their first language. Advocacy and casework support in the UK is hard enough to get even when English is your first language. In some places there are education and training opportunities to help people looking after dependent older relatives understand the importance of being identified as a carer. It really helps if people have access to social and recreational activities that are culturally appropriate, because these meetings and events are a good place for sharing information about how to get support for caring.

The Bengali women's group has been serving the Rockingham community for nearly thirty years. Its expertise on the needs of the Bengali community is well recognised not only by the locals but also by the surrounding neighbourhood where many ... have been rehoused. Bengali women come to the centre when they need to voice concerns, understand expectations and learn how to best help themselves and their family. (Bengali Women's Group in Southwark)

Even if there is a family member who is fluent in both the language of the older person and English, it can be very difficult to explain a lot of terms that are used by doctors and social workers. It is also difficult emotionally to be sympathetic and understanding as a carer while also translating the decisions and predictions of doctors. A specialist link worker with knowledge of a particular disease would help. For example, knowing about cancer and having an ability to interpret all of the medical terms that may come up in a consultation is massively helpful in supporting carers through the illness and treatment of their loved one.

An experienced specific ethnic community worker can help families to understand the condition and manage the symptoms of whichever illness or disability the person is experiencing. This enables the people affected, their partners, families and carers to be fully informed and plan the pathway through care and, where possible, recovery. It also helps with planning for future decision-making. Peer support is very important, and it's only through the community that real peers can be found.

Carers may be fortunate where there are residential care facilities appropriate to their family's culture. This is more likely in urban areas. In more remote or rural areas or even in small towns these are less likely to be available. But it is important to know that even then the personal space in a care home can be modified with familiar decorations and furniture, and appropriate menus must be provided by the care operator. As a family you can work with the people providing care to make sure that life is as comfortable as possible in residential care.

Some communities are more likely than others to regard enlisting professional care from outside the home as a failure of family responsibility. It's important to help people understand that they can continue to provide essential caring support while allowing care workers to do some of the work. Everything has changed since the times we may remember from the past, when family care at home was the only way. It may no longer be the best way to provide the best-quality care for older family members in every case.

'Self-directed support' is described in more detail in the Big List in Chapter Seven. It emphasises the importance of choice, control and flexibility in the care that is received, which is of particular value for people who find mainstream support services unresponsive.

There is an introduction to self-directed support in Scotland on the website of MECOPP. That's a charity that works in partnership with

*others to challenge and dismantle barriers that deny minority ethnic
carers access to health, social work and other social care services.
This self-directed support allows people to access support that's better
suited to their specific cultural and or religious needs. (Social worker)*

There is help if you can find it. More contacts are in Useful Contacts and Resources.

LGBT+ carers

There are an estimated 1 million LGBT+ people over the age of 55
in the UK. They have been described in 2018 in YouGov research
as being nearly twice as likely to expect to rely on health and
social care services and paid-for help when they become older.

Because many older people are not comfortable with being
'out' to care home staff, hospital staff, paid care, social workers
or their housing provider, the position of the friend or partner
who is a carer is made awkward. If the one you care for is not
'out', then who are you? And what rights do you have? It is still
reported that people who are living with an illness like dementia or another disability face double stigma associated with both
their condition and their sexual identity. A survey by the LGBT+
campaigning organisation Stonewall in 2015 reported that up to
25 per cent of patient-facing staff have heard colleagues making
homophobic, biphobic or transphobic remarks. That is not a
comforting statistic for carers.

Support services can make well-intentioned assumptions
which are unhelpful and trigger distressing recollections of discrimination. Older gay and lesbian carers seeking support may
encounter prejudice or misunderstanding even when professionals mean to be open and accepting. In recent years training and
awareness of the health and social care issues for older people

from the LGBT+ community has been improved by the charity Opening Doors, working in partnership with other care and ageing organisations. This organisation provides accredited training to professionals and conducts research. They connect people over the age of 50 with activities and events, support and information across the UK but mainly in London. Age UK has made a resource pack for professionals about meeting the needs of older lesbian, gay, bisexual and transgender people who are using health and social care services which includes this quote:

The staff in the home rarely gave us any time alone together and on one occasion Arthur was taken seriously ill and transferred to hospital without them notifying me. The man I love could have died and I wouldn't have been there or even known. (Ian)

A 2010 survey by Stonewall found that lesbian, gay and bi people were more likely to be single and to live alone, and less likely to have children or see family members.

Throughout this book there are many references to younger-generation family members supporting older relatives. That sort of support is not available to people estranged from their families or who are child-free.

I cried when I watched the Russell T. Davies TV series It's a Sin *about HIV at the end of the last century. I remember how awful it was when people I knew were whisked away from loved ones by families at the end of life. (Former HIV/AIDS adviser)*

It is still happening in this century. It is not uncommon for blood relatives to become suddenly more involved towards the end of a person's life when they have had very little contact or relationship in recent years. There is evidence that they have often been given more regard by the hospital or care home authorities than has the lover or friend who is much closer to the person but who has no recognised status. Getting registered as the carer is essential. It gives the carer formal standing, which they would not have if they were asked whether they were 'next of kin'.

I felt pity for him when I asked Clive who was his next of kin, and he told me that he doesn't have any kin. That seemed so sad. But he laughed out loud and told me that he had lived with the same man for thirty years and he was waiting outside to come in and visit as soon as possible because they couldn't bear to be apart. In future I'm never going to ask about next of kin. I'm just going to ask who we should tell if anything happens and if there is someone we should keep informed in the meantime. (Hospital nurse)

The creation of civil partnerships and same-sex marriages in recent years has offered another formal status that must be recognised by health and social care services. If you are 'just' a friend, then it's important that those providing care ask the person who they feel closest to and who they would like to be involved in decisions and given information about their care needs. And if you get power of attorney sorted and get registered as the carer, then you cannot be overridden by anyone, not even long-lost relatives appearing on the scene.

LGBT+ people now have greater protection in law than at any time in history. They are entitled to services that are inclusive. The legislation involved is the Equality Act 2010 which replaced anti-discrimination laws with a single Act. This law helps to tackle discrimination and inequality. It applies to all organisations that provide a service to the public or a section of the public. Sexual orientation, sex and age are all protected characteristics which are covered by the Act.

Male carers

Although they are fewer in number than women, there are still over 2.5 million men in the UK who are carers. It appears that men who are carers are much less likely than women to reach out for support, for example from carers' groups. The support from meeting people in a similar situation is significant, both for practical tips and advice about local services, but also friendship. Persuading people who are currently carers to meet with others in a support group is a major hurdle. Apart from the fact that all carers are busy, and that finding someone to cover for you while you go to a group is a challenge, men are probably less likely to regard themselves as carers than women. During the COVID-19 pandemic it seemed that men's groups flourished because it was easier for men to use technology to keep in touch than to come to meetings. But face-to-face meetings will have their place again.

I attended a meeting, in a semi-rural area, of men married to women affected by dementia. Their meeting started with some practical help and advice about local services from a district nurse. And then it became more of a discussion group. There was a lot of joking and teasing of each other. This is very typical of Scottish guys. At one point one of the gentlemen looked as if he was going to become emotional about an incident that had happened, and the men closed around him in quite an amazing demonstration of comradeship which ended up with laughter and plans to go to the pub. (Community psychiatric nurse)

A report commissioned by the Carers Trust found that more than half of the male carers felt that men find it hard to ask others for help and support, and for them as much as women balancing work and caring is challenging. A significant number of the employed men who were asked said they'd not say that they were carers to anyone, which means they are cut off from any support that might be available through the workplace. There is clearly an effect on men's health, as on women's. Male carers visit their GP much more than other men do. There is more about the health of carers in Chapter Five.

Long-distance carers

Trying to take care of ageing people from a distance is hard. It doesn't matter whether the carers are in a different country or just a couple of hours away. They can end up spending a lot of time and money on travel. And even if they are giving up all they can afford, long-distance carers can be affected by stress and guilt about how much they are able to do. Carers who support from far away are sometimes called 'remote carers'.

Even without visiting at all there are still very important tasks to undertake or contributions to make. Financial help for the person they care for or those who are doing most of the day-to-day caring can make a big difference. They may take over administrative tasks such as organising the paying of bills and managing finances online. They can provide long-distance support to the friends and neighbours or other family members who are able to visit and bring meals. They can thank them, doing so in a way that isn't patronising. Everyone loves a bunch of flowers or some other treat through the post.

Depending on their skills, they can be the person who does the research on the options if it is time to think about respite care or residential care. Even when it comes to home mainte-nance, like getting a workman to put in a new boiler or fix the roof, they may have the knowledge and time to research local trusted traders and organise those tasks at long distance. People are becoming confident in using Skype, FaceTime or Zoom for family gatherings now. Any long-distance carer can help to organise those meetings and support the working-out of a plan of action that fits the skill sets and availability of all the other people involved.

Planning visits is crucial. It's important that long-distance carers go to see the family member at some time if humanly possible. It's helpful if they co-ordinate with the main carer on the timing of the visit. That visit may present an opportunity to give the main carer a break, so just dropping in might turn out to be annoying rather than a benefit. Letting everyone know when the long-distance carer is going to come gives them a chance to plan. If there are a number of long-distance carers, WhatsApp is a very useful phone app to make sure that everyone can spread out visits in the interest of the loved one, and also give each other information about anything they see that needs doing when they're there.

Other carers

The description of carers in this chapter is not exhaustive. Everyone is different, but you may identify with some of those outlined here. The one thing they have in common is an older person who needs help.

Chapter 2

Why might an older person need care?

Almost 1.5 million people in the UK are aged over 85, and this number is expected to double in the next twenty years. (FCA 2015 Paper No. 8)

Before exploring why an older person might need care, a word of caution. Not every older person needs care. It's nice to be cared *about*, but being cared *for* only comes when things get difficult. Lots of older people are fit and well. Old age must not be defined by what someone cannot do. On the contrary, it must be defined by what they can do. At the time of writing, older celebrities like Dame Judi Dench and Sir Patrick Stewart in their eighties continue to work and entertain people. Hillary Clinton is still active in politics in her seventies, along with Donald Trump and Joe Biden. And there are American senators in their eighties – Nancy Pelosi for example. Queen Elizabeth II is still working in her nineties. There are Members of the UK Parliament in their seventies and one in his eighties. You can be old and in your prime.

According to his profile on the Asia Pacific Hospice Palliative Care Network, a medical doctor, Dr Hinohara, age 105, was still working.

… it is not uncommon for [Hinohara] to stay up until 5 a.m. to write, sleep for an hour and then get up, drink a glass of milk and a cup of coffee before going about his appointments for the day.

Apart from extraordinary public figures and international celebrities, there are very many older people still working quietly in their family business, at a local job or volunteering. *Guinness World Records* highlights an Italian-born New York resident, Anthony Mancinelli, who died at 108 years old and was the oldest working barber in the world. A McDonalds restaurant in Evansville, Indiana, boasted of a 94-year-old woman still working part-time on the early shift. In 2018 the NHS celebrated the retirement of Monica Bulman, who worked in nursing from the age of 19 until she was 84. Very many older people have vital roles within their families, in childcare and other domestic duties, teaching skills to generations that follow them. BBC local radio regularly features people such as Dorothy Barnett, a hospice shop volunteer aged 99. She had always worked in a business and she loves meeting people. Saying that she wants to work 'until He calls me', she hopes that won't happen before she reaches 100. Keeping working, says Dorothy, is the secret to a long and healthy life.

There is clear evidence worldwide that humans are living better for longer. The United Nations calls our increased longevity one of the most significant social transformations of the twenty-first century. Even in low-income countries where people are likely to live to 60 years of age for the first time in history, there is a new definition of old age. Dementia, the alarming condition that has (according to research) replaced cancer as the disease that scares us most, is not increasing as fast as predicted. There are over half a million people over the age of 100 in the world. Almost 100,000 of them are in the US. As of January 2022, the oldest person in the world was a Japanese woman of 119. Of the European countries, France, Spain and Italy have the highest number of people over 100. The number of centenarians is growing fast, and it has been estimated that one-third of babies born in the UK in 2013 will live to be 100.

The world is a safer place for most people in high-income countries, and more of us are benefiting every day from improved nutrition, sanitation, disease control, new medicines, road safety, education, safer housing ... the list is endless. It means that fewer people die young of avoidable causes. They live to be old.

The progress has not levelled people up yet. There is still a scandal of differentials between poor and rich people within any country. For example, in Scotland there is a difference of as much as ten years of life expectancy between two neighbouring districts near the city of Glasgow, the more affluent Bearsden and the less affluent Drumchapel. But overall we are all living for longer. Many more people now live into old age than in the past. It is concerning, though, that according to the World Health Organization (WHO) in its 2015 *World Report on Ageing and Health*, older individuals were not necessarily living healthier or more active lives. They launched a 'Decade of Healthy Ageing' plan in response starting 2020. This recognises that there is a continued and increasing need for health and social care. Families and friends will continue to be relied upon to provide caring support. An intervening crisis like COVID-19 doesn't help the implementation of such an ambitious plan, and it remains to be seen how it will work.

Everyone is different, and though they are unusual, there are examples of people who are super-fit at a great age.

I am not talking fashion or glamour model stereotypes here. I am talking about the body we all know to be great when we see it ... For me, an excellent shape is an upright body without excess fat, a good waistline, a flattish front and toned from tip to toe. (Norma Williams, fitness fan, 70)

Norma is extremely fit, exercises and is careful of her diet, and runs a business. But any women in their seventies and over can continue to live well if they are able to focus on a healthy life-style. This means regular physical activity every day.

Joan MacDonald, a 74-year-old Canadian fitness influencer, spent the last few years improving her health. She had been suffering from symptoms of high blood pressure and arthritis that were affecting her life. She started making changes because she was unwell and now she is well and helping others to get fit.

Three years ago, I began this long, slow journey and now I realise that there really isn't any end to it. At any moment we can make a decision to change. No matter how difficult or challenging life is, we must remain steadfast in our aim and keep inching forward. (Joan MacDonald)

Normal ageing

Towards the end of our longer lives, a few things may start to need attention. Humans are not exactly like machines, but unfortunately, as with an old appliance, component failures will occur after long use. Some worn parts of humans can be surgically replaced with manufactured components such as hips, knees and artificial lenses. Metabolic changes are harder to fix. Diabetes is one of the chronic conditions that is putting a burden on individuals, their families and health systems. Like many other chronic conditions, such as dementia, there are lifestyle factors which, if adopted, might delay the onset or reduce the severity of the condition and the need for care. But because the risk always increases with age, the number of people affected will rise along with the ageing of the population.

There are changes that have always been associated with age. These include impairment of hearing or eyesight. Or it could be a loss of muscle strength, or a mobility problem caused by arthritis. Technology and medication can sometimes help, but not always. Older people tire more easily. Any one of these issues can make life much harder, let alone an accumulation of them. In the end, we may need extra help with everyday living from that point until we die. We want to stay as well as possible for as long as possible, but at any time your health might break down. There may be care available at home, but sometimes a person may have to take up residential care. What are the things that make a difference and lead anyone to need care? And why is care at home sometimes no longer possible?

When you ask me why anyone needs residential care, it boils down to three things. First, they can't do some important things for themselves, like organise their meals or go to the toilet. Second, they don't live with someone who can take care of that for them or don't have someone near enough to provide enough care all of the time. Night and day. Third, and this is the remarkable thing, they have some incident that draws them to the attention of the authorities. It could be a fall, an infection, an accident or just a neighbour expressing concern. At that point, especially if they end up in a hospital, the usual exit door is into residential care. (Nurse)

Whether the person returns home, goes to live with relatives, or in sheltered accommodation (assisted living) or even in a care home, the role of the informal carer increases each year if the person becomes more frail or disabled.

Although some people may be able to reverse some of the symptoms of ageing and keep disability at bay by making a sustained and focused effort, it can prove impossible for others. The normal ageing process is associated with a small decline in functional ability each year. Sitting too much and not exercising accelerates those normal changes which include:

- Reduction in muscle mass and increase in body fat leading to reduction in strength. This makes falling more likely.

- Reduction in bone mass, and increased joint problems, so that if a person does fall they are more likely to break bones.

- Reduction in blood volume, so that blood pressure control is reduced, for example leading to faintness when the person stands up.

- Changes in the kidneys and changes in whether you feel thirst, so that you are more likely to become dehydrated which in itself can give rise to infections and other problems that make the person confused and dizzy, leading to trips and slips.

- Reduction in lung capacity, so you get out of breath more, making exercise harder so you miss out on the benefits of exercise.

- Visual and hearing impairment.

- Changes in the brain and nervous system, including slower thinking and reflexes. This also affects the autonomic nervous system, i.e. the nerves that control functions you don't think about controlling in the ordinary way such as your heartbeat, digestion and temperature.

- Reduced activity in your bowel leading to constipation, which can even affect your thinking.

- Changes in your liver that make a difference to how your body responds to medicines and alcohol.

- Reduced calcium absorption because your body is less sensitive to vitamin D, so you are more prone to infections, fatigue, depression, bone problems and hair loss.

What causes disability in older people?

'Disability' is a word that is used to describe a wide range of issues. It includes the physical impairments a person might have. Age doesn't come alone. As we are growing from childhood to adulthood we get physically stronger, but eventually that process starts to reverse. This is especially true in people who have not been able to exercise or pay attention to their nutrition, and those who have had illnesses or accidents that reduced their physical strength. As a result, there may be problems in later life doing the things they used to be able to do. That's sometimes called 'acquired disability'. At other times it refers to problems that the person has had all their life, but which may become more pronounced with age as the person's resilience is decreased. That impairment might significantly affect the person's capacity to do things for themselves or act independently.

It is vital to remember that this is not entirely down to the individual's health or their level of fitness. It is a complex interaction between the person and their own environment. Sometimes the environment is almost entirely to blame. A person living on the top floor of a building who has difficulty with stairs is fine for as long as the lift to their flat is working. Someone who can't reach up high above their head will be OK if all their cupboards are at a reasonable height. A little step stool might help, but if they become unsteady on their feet, that bit of furniture itself becomes a health hazard. Ability is a balance of features of the person's physical capacity and features of their environment. We create 'inability' or 'impossibility' that amounts to the same thing as 'disability', particularly for older people. Infrastructure issues, like whether you can order goods by telephone and get groceries delivered, or whether there is public transport, can make the difference between a person having 'disability' or not.

Even where there is public transport, research has revealed that passengers are more likely to be looking down at their phones than looking up to see if anyone older and less able needs a seat. Older people may worry so much about not getting a seat that they are less likely to use the bus. It increases the risk of isolation as they don't get out and about, but also increases the need for carers to do things for them.

All too often we hear of people struggling to access their local shops and leisure facilities because of a lack of seating areas to rest in ... we want to see older people enjoy their lives to the fullest. For this reason, Standing Up 4 Sitting Down is calling on retailers and high streets to do their bit to improve the lives of people by providing adequate seating in stores and public spaces. There are now over 2,000 retail outlets ... pledging to maintain the number of seats people can use if they want to rest mid-shop. (Anchor Hanover)

And it is not just about muscles and bones. Sensory impairment, i.e. problems with hearing and sight, can make life more difficult if not corrected. Cognitive impairment is almost impossible to reverse, so extra support is needed. That impairment is when the person cannot think as efficiently or clearly as they used to. It might show up as no longer being able to find the words for objects or concepts, becoming lost in familiar places, and not recognising people. All older people seem to have some cognitive slowing and even mild cognitive impairment, and in some cases – but not all cases – this progresses to full-blown dementia.

When any notion of disability is being discussed by professionals in respect of the person you care for, you will hear reference to 'activities of daily living' (often shortened to ADLs). This term covers personal care activities like eating, dressing, going to the toilet and personal hygiene such as showering or having a bath. It is worth remembering about ADLs because as a carer you may often be asked about them, and which of them the person you care for needs help with. Another definition is IADLs (you will notice that care systems do like acronyms), which stands for 'instrumental' activities of daily living. This includes managing medication, doing housework, shopping, looking after money and keeping on top of personal paperwork like banking, insurance, bills etc. These may be influenced by both physical impairments and cognitive impairments.

My dad took care of all the finances, and when he died Mum struggled. She used to go to the local branch of the bank, and the staff there were kind and helpful. However, the branch closed, and she cannot get to grips with digital banking, so I've had to take that off her. (Daughter of Niamh, 92)

Now that the branch is closed, this lady has been disabled because she doesn't have the resilience to learn how to do her banking on a computer or smartphone. She might not even own one of these. She has been 'instrumentally' disabled.

Another important concept in caring for older people is 'frailty'. Although this word is often used in ordinary conversations, it now has a technical medical definition. The WHO defines frailty very specifically.

Frailty manifests as increased vulnerability, impaired capability to withstand intrinsic and environmental stressors, and limited capacity to maintain physiological and psychosocial homeostasis. Frailty is found in 20–30 per cent of the elderly population aged over 75 years and increases with advancing age. It is associated with long-term adverse health-related outcomes such as increased risk of geriatric syndromes, dependency, disability, hospitalisation, institutional placement and mortality.

In other words, looking at it from the positive side, after age 75 almost three-quarters of us are *not* frail. The risk of frailty increases over time, though, if the person accumulates deficits. If you are likely to become their carer, keeping the person you care for as well as possible for as long as possible is important. The frailer they become, the greater your task and the earlier it will become necessary to provide additional caring support such as residential care. You want to avoid those deficits or delay them. The aim is to reduce dependency.

And if you yourself are a carer, especially as you get older, you need to make sure to care for yourself as much as anyone else. There is more about this in Chapter Five.

Miss B was in her seventies, and she had worked her fingers to the bone for about ten years looking after her father after she retired. He died at 99, and she did not even reach her eightieth birthday. I think she had worn herself out. (GP)

If someone is in need of a carer, the chances are that they have some or all of the problems that give rise to increased frailty risks.

Health problems that lead to frailty or disability requiring care

Illness can cause disability. According to research, five types of chronic illnesses cause much of the disability in older people after age 65. These include:

- Foot problems. A good geriatrician, or physician for older people, will start their assessment of an older person by getting their shoes and socks off. Very many foot problems in older people can be improved by shoe modification and the use of cushioned insoles. As you get older the padding under your feet decreases, which can cause pain in the ball of the foot and heels. Toenails may become thickened and difficult for the older person to cut, especially if bending over is hard and the person has lost some of the strength in their hands to use scissors or clippers. Fungal nail infections are common. Some of the other common painful troubles include bunions, corns, calluses and ingrowing toenails. All these problems can make the person less able or willing to walk, and walking is very important for all the tasks that keep you independent, as well as being good for general health. The podiatrist is a friend indeed.

- Arthritis. Osteoarthritis is the most common form of arthritis in older people. It causes joint stiffness and pain that can be mild or excruciating. The joints may become swollen and tender, and there may be a crunching feeling or even a sound as bones rub together. It can affect the hands, knees, hips and spine. Daily activities such as walking, climbing stairs, getting in and out of the bath, getting dressed and taking care of your feet become difficult. There is no treatment that cures this and it can cause significant disability in older people, although pain can be managed, and knowing about aids to reduce disability can transform your work of caring for someone. There is more about accessing aids in the Big List in Chapter Seven under 'Equipment for household tasks'.

- Cognitive impairment. Losing some mental capacity is not inevitable with age, but the risk increases as the years go by. Many older people have mild cognitive impairment that stops them being as sharp as they used to be, but which does not progress to a significant extent. In some cases the person goes on to develop dementia, which means that they are not able to look after themselves or their affairs as well as they used to.

Getting lost or confused and not being able to handle money or communicate well all cause increasing problems over time. There is no cure, but there are lifestyle changes that can help delay the progress of this condition. If you know about these changes your burden of care may decrease. There are useful publications listed at the end of the book, in particular *Dementia: The One-Stop Guide*.

● Heart problems. Older people are at increased risk of cardiovascular disease – problems with the blood vessels and the heart. Physical activity and other lifestyle issues such as diet, smoking and drinking alcohol make a difference to the level of risk. There are drug therapies that can help. Signs include chest pain, pressure and discomfort, but any general problems doing normal activities could be related to a heart problem, even headaches, dizziness and confusion or just tiredness. Blood pressure, diabetes and cholesterol control are important for heart health. Also stress management.

● Visual impairment. Loss of sight in older people is a major health problem. Common problems are short sight, cataracts, age-related macular degeneration, glaucoma and diabetic retinopathy. In cataracts, where the lens of the eye becomes cloudy, vision can be restored with surgery. If visual impairment is not treated it increases the risk of falls, which can leave the person with a disability, and if it leads to hospital treatment there are added risks. The person may start to lose their independence and their confidence to live alone. They may become socially isolated and afraid to go out and about, leading to depression. All older people should have an eye examination every year or two to treat problems and prevent permanent visual loss. If the person you care for has visual impairment, you need to know about all the aids and adaptations that can help them to be more independent. Note that the optician will come and visit at home and tests are free for older people.

Other common problems in older people include:

- Hearing impairment. Hearing loss affects about a third of people by the time they are seventy, and more than 80 per cent by the time they are 85. It is an effect of age, but there are many conditions that can cause hearing problems that can be fixed, such as ear wax or medications that affect the ear. Older people should get regular assessment and hearing can be made the best it can be with hearing aids, assistive listening devices and rehabilitation programmes. After high blood pressure and arthritis, hearing loss is the most common problem in older people. And a common problem with the hearing aid is not knowing how to switch it on and maintain it.

- Chronic heart and lung problems. Shortness of breath, a chronic cough and not being able to keep up with usual activities should be checked out in older people, particularly when accompanied by loss of appetite and fatigue. Some heart problems feel like stomach problems, so heartburn or indigestion might actually be coming from heart disease. In older age the heart may become too weak or stiff to pump blood around the body as before, causing breathlessness and swollen ankles, but medication can control this for years. However, you need to see the doctor.

- Falls and hip fractures. Anyone can have a fall but older people are more vulnerable, especially if they have a long-term health condition. There are ways the risk can be reduced, including simple changes in the home and doing strength and balance exercises. An older person might faint from standing up too quickly, from being too hot, or not eating and drinking enough.

In the UK falls are the most common cause of injury-related deaths in people over the age of 75. Any of the health problems listed above can increase the risk of a fall.

Later in this book there is some advice on dealing with practical problems arising from any of these issues. First it is important to consider to what extent those illnesses are inevitable, and if not, how they can be prevented. Although they are more common in older people, they should not be accepted as an inevitable part of growing old. Some things can be done to delay them, and lots can be done to get round them.

How to control or delay normal ageing problems

You can't stop ageing while you are alive, obviously. Every day you are automatically one day older. But it is possible to manage some of the problems that are more common in older people. The problems listed above can often be modified with lifestyle changes or with support from your medical adviser or GP. But the doctor can't help you if your problems are not brought to her attention. Many older people, especially men, are reluctant to see the doctor to ask about problems at an early stage. Often they wait until it is too late to benefit from the treatments and even cures that are available.

Getting a health assessment

Older patients are entitled to a regular check-up from their GP. If the person you care for has not been called for such a check, it is worth getting in touch with the doctor to find out if it can be arranged. Sometimes the problem doesn't appear until the person has attended the doctor for another reason.

Dad had been feeling tired and was losing weight, so we went to see the doctor because I wondered if he was developing diabetes. The doctor did a full blood test and discovered that he had diabetes as suspected, but also a problem with his prostate. That was how we discovered he had prostate cancer. He had avoided going to see the doc for a routine prostate check because he didn't fancy the idea of the rectal exam. If he had waited for much longer, he might not be with us now. (Arnold, son of Geraint, 72)

Going into hospital

Any of the problems that are more common in older people can become worse if the person has an episode of illness or requires a time in hospital. Sometimes the impression is given that hospital stays reveal problems that were already there, but it is now accepted going into hospital can be bad for an older person and cause new problems.

Older people are significantly at risk of developing delirium if they are admitted to hospital. This is a condition that can last for a long time and looks a lot like dementia – the difference being that it is reversible, unlike dementia. There is more about delirium in Chapter Seven. The longer a patient stays in hospital, the more chance there is of catching a hospital-acquired infection. Research shows that there can be a decline in the older patient's mental and physical health, with an irreversible reduction in their quality of life as a consequence of a hospital stay. It may be due to a combination of stress, noise, sleeplessness, dehydration, immobility and not eating properly, not to mention loneliness and boredom. There is more in the 'Hospitals' section of Chapter Seven about supporting loved ones. An investment of time during a hospital admission can make your job of caring afterwards much lighter.

However, a hospital admission is also an excellent opportunity for an older patient to have a thorough check-up, if they've not already had one at home. This is sometimes called a CGA (Comprehensive Geriatric Assessment). Assessment of how anyone is able to look after themselves is usually done better in the person's own domestic environment. How you perform in your pyjamas in a hospital might be quite different from how you do at home in your day clothes. What you need to be able to do is very particular to your home environment. It depends on steps and stairs, heating and lighting, any support you have, the sort of neighbourhood you live in and a whole range of things that can't be replicated in the hospital setting. Never the less, for older patients there ought to be a comprehensive assessment at the time of any crisis that requires hospital admission, including:

● **Treatment of unstable medical conditions.** The person might be discovered to have a condition that had not been detected such as heart failure, or a metabolic disease like diabetes or thyroid problems.

● **Sorting any treatable problems contributing to disability.** There may be simple solutions to undetected problems, such as visual and hearing impairments, mouth problems that affect eating, foot problems that could be corrected with orthopaedic inserts or shoes, or simple help with cutting toenails.

My dad had seemed more and more confused but when we got him to hospital after his fall, they discovered that his ears were completely blocked with earwax. The nurse explained that especially when someone lacks their back teeth and can't chew properly, wax can build up unnoticed. Everyone thinks the person has gone vague or depressed and passive, but all along they've been going deaf. (Daughter of John, 92)

Hospitals can find out things that make life better. However, remember the risks for older people in hospital and the hints in Chapter Seven.

Reviewing existing medicines

It is not safe to stop medications without advice. However, there are high-risk medications and high-risk combinations of medications that can make an older person worse, rather than better. Researchers describe a 'prescribing cascade', which is where one medicine has a side effect, and more medicine is given for that effect. Too many medicines. As your kidneys and liver get older, they don't metabolise your medicines as they once did. Sometimes things that look like problems of ageing can be reversed by stopping some of the medications.

But even if it seems the treatment is no longer making a difference, withdrawal requires careful planning and monitoring to make sure that there is no harm caused. One thing that might often be added is vitamin D, which is important for older people, especially if they don't get out in daylight much. It contributes to bone strength, which you want to maintain in people who might fall over.

Medication is usually reviewed when someone is in hospital, but you can ask for this at any time at home from the local pharmacist. Deprescribing is the process of reducing the number of drugs taken at any time. Age UK estimates that almost 2 million people over 65 are likely to be taking at least seven prescribed medicines. With a review it is likely that some of those can be stopped for the benefit of the patient.

Early mobilisation

The national 'End PJ Paralysis' drive was launched by the English Chief Nursing Officer in 2018.

'Pyjama paralysis' is a loss of strength and function caused by long periods of bed rest. Not getting dressed into day clothes can make you feel like you should stay in bed all day and not actively take part in recovery programmes.

Hospitals are great for fixing people up, but there is a huge amount that can be done to help that process. This includes keeping as mobile as possible in hospital. Lying and sitting still for long periods is bad for people. If you are visiting an older person in hospital, it is a good idea to check if you are permitted to take them for a walk. If that is not possible, arm and leg movements can be done while sitting in the chair. If the person you care for loses condition while in hospital, your job of caring is increased after they come home.

Nutritional support

One important measure is regular weighing and responding to changes in weight. Lots of things can lead to malnutrition. Older people may eat less because of poor oral health and difficulties in chewing and swallowing, but equally it may be psychological. Eating is a social activity, and loneliness and depression can reduce the desire to eat. The effort required to prepare meals may be too much, and some medications cause loss of appetite. It is very complicated and not always understood in every case. When someone is in hospital they should be weighed as part of the assessment, but this is something that you can do at home as well. From time to time, you may notice a loss of weight because clothes don't fit any more. Having a note of what the person used to weigh is very useful information for working out what is going on.

Chapter Seven: The Big List provides hints and ideas for how you as a carer can help with the practical problems that arise from normal ageing and from illness, disability or frailty. Subjects are arranged in alphabetical order for ease of reference.

Chapter 3

Money

The cost of care

The cost of care is not just about the money of the person being cared for. Caring for someone creates financial pressures for the carer. The emotional and health cost of caring is explored in other parts of this book. This chapter is focused mainly on the financial cost of caring which falls on the carer. It's all about money – how to manage it and how to source it. It also examines how people feel about money, because financial conversations are difficult in any relationship at the best of times. When the relationship is shifting so that one person is gradually giving up control and the other may be taking it over, discussions about money can be challenging.

Is it money for you that is needed or for the person you care for? If it is money for them to pay for their care, you may find helpful advice in *Care Homes: The One-Stop Guide*. The person being cared for must pay for their own care where it is provided by professionals. The private care home or private care provider in their own home must charge the older person receiving their services. That makes sense. They are businesses. But it is sometimes a surprise that even care organised or provided to an older person by the council must be paid for by the older person, if they can afford to pay. It is means-tested. That is, the council asks about what money the old person has, and that person must spend quite a lot of it before the council will stop charging them for services and provide free ones. The carer is not liable for those costs. As a carer, you might be involved in helping the older person work out what they must pay for and how, but you don't have to provide that money. What money you have is yours. It's painful when the person cared for or their family didn't realise that elder care provided by professional carers is only free when the person doesn't have the means to pay for it. Carers some-times subsidise the care by paying 'top-up' money to the council or care home provider. But that is purely voluntary.

What about the financial demands that are made on the carer? You might be spending without realising, and spending more than you can afford. It just creeps up on you.

There is some financial support for carers described in this chapter. The advice in any printed book is best for signposting the reader through the confusion of places where you can get live information. The situation about tax and benefits changes almost with every annual government Budget so you need to keep up to date. There is usually local variation, not just between England, Scotland, Wales and Northern Ireland but also between local authority areas in each of those four countries of the United Kingdom. Added to that, there are smaller charities that operate in very specific geographical areas, and finding out if you are lucky enough to live in an area covered by a local foundation can be time-consuming. There are also supports for people with specific characteristics, like veterans, or people of a particular religious faith. Anyone would need help finding a way through this maze.

You may not realise how much financial pressure your caring is putting you under. Some spending may be obvious, like when you use your own cash or card to buy someone's shopping or pay for their entertainment. Perhaps you are in the habit of paying for the teas and coffees when you go out for a few hours. It might not be a lot each time, but it soon adds up.

I used to go with Mum to the coffee shop every Monday and get her a hot chocolate and a bun. Not a big deal really. But with cream and marshmallows! That was £3.35 a pop, and the buns were £3.50. So nearly £7 for Esme every time and not much less for me. Eventually I added it up and realised it was damaging my budget because in a year it added up to over £700. But once we were in the habit it was hard to make it stop. I told her I was on a diet and just had tap water in the café on Mondays after that. (Shirley, daughter of Esme, 82)

Shirley and Esme had a pattern of behaviour that was costing more money than Shirley could afford, and she didn't know how to change that arrangement with her mum other than denying herself the treat.

Some financial pressures are significant but short-term, like when you need to give up work or reduce your hours during a period of looking after someone when they've just come out of hospital. It helps if your employer offers carer's leave or has other carer policies to support you. Longer breaks in your work pattern will have significant long-term financial consequences for you, perhaps delaying any promotion through the ranks of your profession or organisation. Missing pay increases or reducing your pension contributions leads to loss of income far into the future. Some carers retire early to care. These are opportunity costs which you might not think about at the time, but you will become aware that they have made a difference when you look into your own financial affairs later.

There are other 'invisible' costs.

I realised that I was using a lot of fuel in the car going back and forward to Mum's. Then I got a massive garage bill for the suspension

on my car, and realised it was related to the great potholes in the
drive leading to her house though I try to negotiate them slowly. She
sometimes offered to get me some petrol, but I never even thought of
asking her to pay for the damage to my car. In any case, I was too
embarrassed to take petrol money off her. (Shirley, daughter of Esme,
82)

Reluctance to take money from your parent, older relative or
the neighbour you care for is understandable. You might wonder
how it would look to others, and if they'd think you were exploiting them. Even if you don't think about it in this way, taking
money can still change a caring relationship. It doesn't matter
that you are not 'doing it for the money'. There are complicated
feelings involved. With your mother or father, you may be aware
that they did everything they could for you and feel that now it is
your duty to do everything you can for them. You love them so
much, or have such a strong sense of duty, that it never crosses
your mind to count the cost, even if they urge you not to be out
of pocket on their account.

Not being 'paid' to care might present an advantage if it gives
you a feeling of being in control of your caring contribution. It
may encourage you to think that you can pick and choose the
amount of care you give and when, because it is a charitable
thing you are doing out of the goodness of your heart. The
example of Shirley demonstrates that even when the monetary
cost of care is all on you, whether it is cash for outings or wear
and tear on a vehicle, it can still be hard for you to step back from
a unilateral commitment. Why would this be? Maybe deep down
you don't think it is unilateral. You may believe you ought to pay
because you 'owe' these payments.

The way we think about caring for our older family members
is incredibly complicated, and some of the stresses that arise

between family members who think about it differently are out-lined in Chapter Four. One person might think that older family members are entitled to care. But to say, 'You cared for me and now it is my turn' sounds like a transaction, as if there was a con-tract between you. Do you think your parents decided to have children so that there would be someone to take care of them in old age? Even if they did, can this be a binding contract when you had no say in it? Even though in some countries there is a legal obligation to care for elders, that sort of law doesn't exist so far in the UK. Is it not more likely that your parents had children for other reasons or no reason? Wasn't it just part of normal life? It's a fact that in general young people don't think ahead much about their own later life. The result of not thinking about the future is a thread that runs throughout this book. When they were younger, your older relatives and friends may have had no thought for the day when they might need care.

Some older people do not have anyone who feels a duty to care for them. On the other hand, some children are very sensi-tive to the sense of entitlement that their parents may have.

Josephine travels hundreds of miles every month to care for her mother Alice, who believes it is Josephine's job to do that care. I think Alice must have done a proper job on Josephine when she was little, because no matter what anyone says to Josephine, she feels overwhelmed with guilt about Alice if she doesn't do this. Unlike the rest of her family. They don't bother. (Karen, partner of Josephine)

Karen is irritated that the burden is not shared by others. If you are thinking about caring as a loving and willing payback for the care you received as a child, what is your feeling about any brothers and sisters who don't share your way of thinking? Karen thinks that Josephine's brothers have avoided commitment. But maybe Alice never brought up her boys to believe there was one. Does the transaction idea mean that all children have equal responsibilities for care, both in time and money? Or perhaps they should be allowed to have a different model in their head, even if it leaves Josephine with a greater financial burden. How does the idea that any family members are doing care as payback fit with the idea of doing care only for respect, for love or out of altruism? There is no answer to this here, but when contemplating money and any feelings of discomfort that you have, you might find it useful to ask those questions about your own situation.

Older people with capital

Sometimes an older person, even if they have enough resources, is afraid to spend because they've lost connection with price inflation and the cost of living.

My dad always looked after the money, and he left Mum well provided. After he died, I would suggest to Mum that we might do something nice, like take a bus tour to the Lake District. She'd have loved to do that but when she saw it cost a few hundred pounds for the all-inclusive long weekend in a lovely hotel, she'd be put off because it was 'too expensive'. She never put on the heating because she thought the bills were frightening, even though she could easily afford it.
(Andrew, son of Grace, 79)

Sometimes the older person sitting on a comfortable bank balance thinks they don't have money, and sometimes they think they are saving it for you.

Uncle Jim always said there was 'a nice pot of money' waiting for me. I tried to persuade him to spend money on himself, but he lived like a pauper. That partly led to poor health and a nursing home, and all his money was gone before he died. Financially I was worse off because I spent a lot on caring for him. I 'subsidised' the care home fees because the free care I did delayed the date when he went into the care home. That allowed him to preserve his 'pot', but the care home picked it up. I don't care because I've got enough, but he would be spinning in his grave if he knew how little he left to me. (Jean, niece, 52)

So, without a doubt, caring costs. If an older person in need of care takes free care from their family, there is no guarantee that this will preserve the family wealth or inheritance. Part of the dilemma about whether to spend money on the person cared for is resolved if you think of it like this: you are not subsidising the person but subsidising the system. Some of the embarrassment about taking money from your older relative is dispelled if you think of it as taking money from the pocket of the local authority or commercial care provider, who will charge them for care later. You have no responsibility to them, however responsible you feel for your older relative.

Let your mum pay for the beverages and buns and take the petrol money she offers. It doesn't mean you are exploiting her. (Shirley's pal, June)

Allowing older people to pay their way is different from encouraging someone to deliberately get rid of resources, as when the person gives away significant parts of their money or their house to prevent having to pay for care. It is known as 'deprivation of assets'. The local authority or tax authorities demand that back if it looks like a deliberate move. It they conclude that you have reduced your assets with the aim of avoiding care fees, they can choose to calculate the fees as if the older person still owned the assets. There would be no point in Alice giving Shirley a lump sum or passing over her house in the run-up to needing care. Shirley might only have to give it back. The family dilemma there is how soon you should give your worldly goods to the next generation to avoid being accused of hiding your wealth.

If you are assessed as having capital you don't actually possess, you will be charged accordingly. The outcome of this may be that the council decides not to fund your care home fees.

The council can't refuse to provide someone with the care they need because they have notional capital. They have a statutory duty to meet the care needs that the person is assessed as requiring.

However, they will assess the charge payable using your notional income and will try to recover the charge from you or seek to transfer the liability for the charges. (Care Information Scotland, outlining a position from The National Assistance (Assessment of Resources) Regulations 1992 that apply throughout the UK)

Seeking 'to transfer liability for the charges' means going after Shirley if her mother's care needs to be funded.

Most people cannot afford to pay for an older family member's care, and even if they could, it is a serious commitment for a long term that is impossible to define. Carers can put themselves in significant financial peril while doing it. Journalists continue to appear astonished at the extent to which the cost of care of older frail people is not covered by the NHS or local authorities. News stories about people with dementia having to sell their homes to pay for care can hardly be described as news because, although this is true, it is scarcely new. Clearly the journalist didn't know about it, but the time when all elder care was paid for through taxation stopped decades ago, when geriatric and psychiatric hospitals were closed down. Even though care-home care was not means-tested for a while, that soon stopped. Care is not free and must be paid for by the person cared for until they have a relatively small amount of money left.

There are political campaigns from time to time to have this changed back to the heady days of the last century, when for about fifty years the state picked up the entire cost, but the demographics of ageing make this a difficult sell for politicians. While there are older people sitting in a small house worth more than the cost of their care, local authorities who struggle to provide social services have little incentive to stop means-testing the elder care that they provide.

The alternative is for everyone else, including poor people and people who don't have older relatives, to pay more tax so that affluent people can keep their houses and their children who never worked for it get a windfall inheritance. It seems odd. If you want your children to be wealthy, give your money with a warm hand. It will do better for them now than later. (Solicitor)

Giving to your family while you are still alive is an alternative to giving with 'a cold hand' after your death. Inter-generational wealth transfer is complicated when wealth is tied up in property such as a house. It is a good idea to talk to a solicitor or independent financial adviser if you have assets you want to protect. It makes sense, if you can help others, to help the next generation while they are having difficulty paying for their education or getting on the housing ladder, and the experts can tell you how to do this most efficiently. But if it is done too late, too close to the time when you may need care, it can be seen as deliberate deprivation. If you accept such a gift, you need to guess that what is given is surplus to what the older person will need to pay for care, because the local authority may come back to you for the cost of that care. The best thing is to think about disposing of your worldly goods early on.

Older people with no capital

However, at least half of older people have nothing to hide because they do not have worldly goods.

Close to 50 per cent of adults do not have the financial stability to cover an unexpected bill of £300. (FCA 2015 Occasional Paper No. 8)

In this position, it is vital to get hold of all the benefits to which both you and the person you care for are entitled. Age UK says that each year up to £3.5 billion of Pension Credit and Housing Benefit goes unclaimed by older people. You want to find out if some of that is yours.

Don't try and navigate this system by yourself. There's the risk of not claiming what you are entitled to. If you erroneously claim what you're not entitled to, you get knocked back and that's dispiriting. If you are a carer, you don't need that hassle after all that time filling forms. We have a benefits adviser who in six months has raised half a million pounds of previously unclaimed benefits. This is because he gently takes people through the system. It takes him two hours to do an Attendance Allowance application form even though he does this process all the time. If you are a carer it takes ten times as long to try to do it yourself. If you are on your knees, you need a gentle soul like him to help you. (Local carers' organisation)

What can be done to help?

There are financial breaks and benefits which may be available to you as a carer and the person you care for, and it is important that you take full advantage of them. Dealing with money and caring is not only about benefits. Managing the finances around caring falls into three main areas with some overlap between them:

1. Helping the person to manage their own finances and eventually taking over

2. Preventing financial harm

3. Securing eligible benefits

1. Helping the person to manage their own finances

Older people are usually well able to manage their own finances, even if they need care in other areas of their life. Any practical difficulties could be as simple as transport or mobility problems that cause trouble getting to the office of a bank, building society or insurance company. Especially now that it is expected that everyone is able to do most of their business online, help may be required if the older person doesn't have a computer or WIFI in the home. Even if they do, they may not have set up digital banking and find that too challenging. So, although they are still in a position to make financial decisions, it is hard for them to implement the decisions without help.

I just wish I could find an 11-year-old who could explain all this to me! (Mary, 72)

Older people in the early stages of dementia will often be able to deal with their own banking even after diagnosis, with increasing amounts of support only required over time. The majority of older people who need care will eventually need some help when using a bank or paying bills. Sometimes it is the muddles with finance that signal the onset of mild cognitive impairment, an early sign of dementia. The banking services sector has produced a charter for people with dementia. The idea is that the banks and related financial services organisations will deliver basic awareness to their customer-facing staff and have a senior person in each department who leads on this. More in-depth training is given to staff who work in teams that deal with vulnerable customers and those dealing with complaints, risk and financial crime.

The best thing about taking Dad to the bank was that the staff had clearly got a note on his file about what he needed as extra support and so we didn't have to go back to the beginning every time we went to a counter. It's a shame that the branch closed. (Jane, daughter with power of attorney for Ian, 92)

Ask your own bank, or get the person to ask their bank, if they provide special help for you as a carer or for the person needing extra support. Banks have to operate within legal constraints and codes which sometimes seem to make life harder for carers, but the charter aims to recognise the needs of carers and support them as 'third parties' to the transactions involving the vulnerable customer. They are meant to understand the provisions within law that allow usually prohibited actions to be undertaken, for example varying the rules around privacy and control of the account. This would include providing alternative security methods to PINs and passwords to reduce the possibility of unnecessary or inappropriate withdrawals from the person's account and keep their money safe.

There is a great deal of advice about managing money on websites such as the Money Advice Service. Banks now offer statements that are easier to read. Longer appointments can be made to see and talk to someone at the bank and there are quiet areas in the bank for meetings. This supports people with dementia and others who are finding it difficult to manage money to do their own banking for as long as possible. It is also helpful for people with visual and auditory impairment, as well as those who just couldn't stand for a long time in a queue or have a personal conversation at a counter through the glass partition. Devices which make life easier for some of us, such as chip-and-pin cards, are a nightmare for people who can't remember numbers. The danger is that such a person would write the number down and keep it with the card, and that means anyone stealing their wallet can have access to their money. Banks won't recompense you if you have revealed your pin number to anyone. However now there are chip-and-signature cards, which allow the person to pay for things in the same way that they may have done many years ago.

When my father started to have difficulty at the bank the staff there made a suggestion which has been really helpful for us. They set us up with a joint account for a little bit of his money so that I could make small routine payments and access funds on his behalf at his request without having to put him through the anxiety of going to the bank every time. Most of his money is still in another account but it doesn't have any bank cards associated with it, so it feels much more secure. If he wants to access it, I can go to the bank with him and he can make any arrangements in discussion with the bank teller. I make sure he always has a bit of cash on him so he can pay his way and get amounts of shopping. (Jane, daughter of Ian, 92)

It is never too soon to discuss this sort of arrangement. If the person that you are likely to care for sets this up at an early stage, then everyone is accustomed to it before the time comes when it must be put into full operation.

Powers of Attorney

The person that you are caring for may reach a position where they are not able to make important financial decisions for themselves. They may increasingly fail to understand or retain the understanding of decisions that need to be made. When that happens, someone must make a proxy decision for them. This impairment in thinking or expressing what they are thinking could be the result of a stroke, mental disorder or dementia. In those circumstances, where someone cannot come to a decision, communicate that decision, understand it, act on it or remember what decision they have made, a health professional can decide whether the person still has some capacity to make decisions or has lost it completely. You must always assume that someone has capacity to make decisions unless there is very clear evidence that they don't.

There is a spectrum. A person who would be unable to manage a complex business decision could still decide when and where to go on holiday. They might even decide to buy ridiculously expensive clothes and perfume. Anyone has a right to make even apparently foolish decisions about things that they can understand. But for major financial decisions that you become unable to make there are robust legal processes that you can set up in advance to make sure that things don't happen that you wouldn't want. Many people are reluctant to think about getting a will and even less so about granting a power of attorney, but this is really important for everyone.

Apart from your own peace of mind, a power of attorney is very helpful to everyone, including family and professionals caring for you if you have lost capacity. Considering setting one up is something that is best done long before the need for care arises. If you are reading this and you've not made one for yourself, investigate that now. In the UK about 26,000 people were seriously injured in road traffic accidents in 2019. Anyone can have an accident. Who would take care of your affairs if you were so unwell for a time that you couldn't be contacted or deal with any of your personal business? It is not only older people who have health incidents requiring someone else to take care of financial affairs for them, if only for a while. You are not giving away power at the moment when you appoint an attorney. It doesn't mean that you have lost control. The person you appoint as your attorney can only deal with your affairs if it has been affirmed that you can't do it yourself. You yourself can also ask them to undertake some of your business before you reach that stage, just for convenience. Once you have one it could lie dormant for decades, but the day you need one it is too late to create one.

Using a power of attorney is frequently associated with dementia.

I knew that getting a power of attorney was important, but it was only when my sister was diagnosed with dementia that I realised the clock was running out for getting this done. We previously left it too late for my father. He reached the stage where a person can't grant a power of attorney any more or make a will because his dementia was too far on. The doctor said he 'lacked capacity'. (Janice, whose sister and father died of early-onset dementia before they were 65)

If no one has been appointed as the attorney in cases like this a court will have to appoint someone, which can be expensive and time-consuming and often at cost to the family.

How do you go about granting a power of attorney? The position is slightly different in each part of the UK. In England a lasting power of attorney (LPA) is a legal document that lets 'the donor' appoint one or more people ('the attorneys' to the donor) to make decisions on behalf of the donor. There are two types of LPA:

- Health and welfare powers
- Property and financial affairs powers

You can choose to make one type of attorney or both. It can be the same person, or (to be on the safe side) more people in case someone has died before you or is not available. The process in Scotland and Northern Ireland is slightly different but has the same aim. You have to choose your attorney, appoint them and register this with the Office of the Public Guardian for each of the countries of the UK (named Office of Care and Protection in Northern Ireland).

To grant a power you can use a solicitor, or you can get forms and information from the Office of the Public Guardian or the Office of Care and Protection. Lawyers charge fees and it is a personal choice to use one or not. Whichever way you do it, the power of attorney must be registered. Doing it on your own depends on your own confidence in these matters. Care UK, the Alzheimer's Society and Alzheimer's Scotland are just some of the organisations that have useful information on their websites about this. You can find those contact details in the Useful Contacts and Resources chapter in this book.

Because we left it too late, we discovered the much more expensive and time-consuming option. We had to go to a court of law to get the authority to make decisions on behalf of our dad. They did say that if no one in the family was prepared to do it then the local authority would do it themselves. Dad would not have liked social workers to have been making decisions on his behalf. (Janice, daughter of man with early-onset dementia)

There is more about powers of attorney, including welfare powers, in the Big List in Chapter Seven. Also recommended is *Power of Attorney: The One-Stop Guide* by Sandra McDonald, the companion volume to this one. This includes information about when these arrangements can go wrong and what to do if you think someone is misusing their powers. Family members sometimes think that the 'wrong' person has been chosen as attorney, and worry that they might abuse the money or just get in a muddle if they are not very businesslike or are too busy.

If someone has broad powers to buy or sell property, manage accounts, handle benefits and tax and deal with debts on your behalf, you need someone who is organised and able to do that. A person might decide to nominate their children to keep it in the family, but you need to be sure that when the time comes they will have the time and personal skills to be able to carry out their duties. You need to think carefully about whether you want to take that on for the person you care for, or if someone else could do it better.

Once a power is registered, it can only be revoked by a court or the person who granted it.

2. *Preventing financial harm*

Financial harm (sometimes referred to as financial abuse) is another name for stealing someone's money or possessions. It is a crime and can include theft, fraud, forgery or embezzlement. Someone might abuse the decision-making powers that they have as an attorney. It includes putting pressure on an older person to make financial decisions they would not otherwise make. There is more awareness now through social media and mainstream media about 'doorstep crime', for example rogue traders and scams on the phone or the internet. There are still scams by post.

Supporting someone else to manage their money is fraught with difficulty, especially if the person is affected by dementia or any other condition that makes it difficult for them to express themselves or to remember what has been discussed. It sometimes feels that financial exploitation is an increasing problem. Or perhaps it is just that it is being more easily detected these days and we are more aware of it.

People with dementia may over time lack judgement and begin to trust the wrong people. Staff in banks, shops and post offices are increasingly trained to notice when customers are struggling with financial transactions. It might even be that they notice before the family does.

I saw the teller in the post office managing a difficult conversation with my mother. I was in the other queue, and they didn't see me. I went over to thank the worker later and she confided that my mother was in there every day of the week asking the same question about her pension. We never knew. (Son of a woman with dementia)

Bank staff are now taught to negotiate with the customer in order to delay a decision if it looks like they are being influenced by an untrustworthy person. But this response is not guaranteed. One daughter told me that her father frequently takes large amounts of money out of the bank in cash, but the next day doesn't have any left to pay for simple things like his newspaper and cigarettes. Her father had his own explanation for why the money was gone.

The boys told me they needed the money from me and came with me to the bank to get it out. (Deirdre, daughter of Ramir, 72)

Deirdre had no clear idea who 'the boys' were but she is aware that locally there are men who furnish Ramir with alcohol and behave as if they are his friend, although they've never been seen around before. It may be that there are unscrupulous people who exploit the vulnerability of the older person before the family has even identified that the vulnerability exists.

Banks are happy to plan with families to try to avoid this sort of difficulty. Things are made simpler for everyone if someone has a financial power of attorney. Previously it may have taken some time to get the bank to understand. They now advertise that they have improved their processes and staff know how to support people who are affected by dementia and to identify possible signs of financial abuse. In the past it may have taken a while to get approval from the bank for a family member to have control over the account, and many rejections were caused by paperwork not being in order. The situation is improving.

Most financial harm and abuse is perpetrated by relatives who often try to justify their actions on the basis that they are claiming inheritance early, or protecting the older person's interests. But it can also be carried out by people who specifically target vulnerable people to exploit them. (Hourglass, an organisation for preventing abuse of older people, formerly known as Action on Elder Abuse)

Sometimes the person you think is exploiting the older person is relatively new in their life, such as a new romantic interest, a new friend or a paid care worker. A monstrous aspect of this is that the older person may be dependent on them or very attached to them. The difference between abuse and ordinary theft is that it is perpetrated by someone who is in a position of trust. This trusting relationship may be relatively recent, as when someone phones up regularly and leads the person to believe that they are now friends. Such targeted abuse is seen differently from opportunism, when a family member might casually use the person's bank card without permission or pressure them into paying for things.

As a carer there are things you can do to spot potential harms:

- Check the person's bank statements regularly.
- Keep an eye on what is spent when others are doing shopping, for example looking at receipts.
- Keep important documents out of sight and make sure people you trust know where they are.

Hourglass has a confidential helpline that provides information and support for anyone concerned about exploitation of an older person. Family, friends, neighbours, professionals or anyone can call 0808 808 8141.

It can be difficult to protect the person you care for from scams.

I had a phone call out of the blue from the insurance company. The nice young person sounded very educated. Anyway, the offer was for renewing the household insurance and it's a special offer, so I had to agree straight away. Then he was asking for my bank details to take a payment and I remembered you told me not to give my pin number and he was most insistent that it was all right. When I told him that I'd have to call you he got rather unpleasant and said that he was cancelling my policy and if the house burns down tonight it would be my fault, and would I just give him the numbers. I'm very worried because it would be a disaster if my insurance has been withdrawn. (Arnold, 92)

This story highlights some of the key elements of a scam. No company should call you out of the blue, and if they do, hang up. It doesn't matter what the person sounds like, you don't do business over the phone with someone you've not met from a company you didn't ring. If they are trying to hurry you, they are not legitimate. Never, ever give pin numbers over the phone or your banking passwords. Your own bank will not ask for them, so if someone is asking, they're not legitimate. Uninvited approaches with exciting offers are too good to be true, so don't be tempted.

You know this, but how do you make sure your older friend or relative does? Just telling them to hang up is not enough. There is good advice from the AARP, a US organisation for older people. They point out that giving stern warnings to older people and trying to control them may cause problems with the relationship. How do you help without hurting their feelings? They suggest some conversations and some actions.

You can't win a contest you didn't enter, Dad. You never have to pay fees to collect lottery winnings, Mum. Government agencies don't make unsolicited phone calls and never ask for personal information – why would they? They've already got it on file ... Remind them what they taught you decades ago: don't trust strangers – especially those seeking personal information and money. (AARP, Protect your Parents from Scams)

In the UK customers have the right to stop their information being used for direct marketing. Less mail makes it easier to spot the bad stuff. You can even put a sign on the door to say 'No Junk Mail'. Some delivery services might ignore that, but you can ask Royal Mail to stop delivering leaflets and brochures to your address. The **Telephone Preference Service (TPS)** is a 'do not call' register for landlines and mobile phones, and registering can reduce unwanted sales calls, but that is only from legitimate businesses and doesn't suppress automated calls. The phone call from a stranger telling you your parcel will be delayed unless you send money may have been routed through a foreign country. Preventing financial harm of older people is extremely complex.

This is where the idea of having their resources split into accessible and less accessible pots is useful, because it can provide damage limitation when something bad happens. The older person will be shocked and ashamed if they are caught out, and the least you can do is keep most of their resources safe.

Many situations are open to different interpretations. If I spend hundreds of pounds on petrol visiting my mum to take care of her, and she seems appreciative and wants to give me money for petrol and for maintaining my car, is that exploiting her? Some actions might be clearly abusive, but others are difficult to sort out. If you are caring for someone and you are taking expenses like this, it is not only important to make sure that the person you care for is happy to pay, but also you can avoid being challenged by making sure there is a clear record and that any other relevant people know about it.

Our mum often gives me a bit of money when I visit, telling me to spend it on the children. I make sure I've told my sister Jen, who also has kids, but she lives a long distance away and never visits. She's told me she thinks it is fair enough. She thinks Mum should give more! I'd not want any more. (Eleanor)

By being open, Eleanor is avoiding the uncomfortable conversation that might take place if Jen discovered accidentally about the gifts. She is giving Jen the opportunity to object and including her in the ongoing conversation about the cost of care and the dilemmas about exploitation and allowing the older person to use their money as they wish. However, it is worth noting that you can claim expenses incurred in carrying out your role as an attorney, for example, travel costs, postage and phone calls. You need to keep a record.

3. Securing eligible benefits

There is one clear answer to the question, 'How do I secure the benefits to which I am entitled?' The answer is that you have to chase and hunt them down.

You won't find the current position in a book, but in an **online benefits calculator**. Looking for guidance and support on benefits for the person you care for can be a long and complicated process, but there are people who can help you and websites that make things easier. Getting advice on benefits is only one aspect of reducing poverty for people who are cared for. The carer has a massive range of things to think about on each of the topics that might be causing concern. Take one question about one of our greatest expenses, fuel. 'My dad doesn't have enough money to keep warm. What can be done?'

I am an adviser and the answer to this isn't only cash benefits but also saving money. I'd be asking if your dad needs his boiler repaired or replaced and whether his house is properly draught-proofed. It is possible that he'd be entitled to a new boiler grant. He might be able to save some money by changing his energy supplier, or even having an energy tariff check with his current supplier. Has he got loft and wall insulation, and is he getting the right winter fuel payments? Is there a local 'Keep Warm' pack for vulnerable older people, and did he get one? That would include items such as a fleece blanket, thermal socks, gloves and a hat. And advice on how to keep warm, like taking hot drinks, heating up only the rooms he is using and dressing warm indoors? I could go on … but so many things depend on whether he is a tenant or owns the house, and what benefits he is already on. Has he had the Cold Weather Payment when the weather is averaging sub-zero for a week? He can get a Warm Home Discount from his supplier which will come automatically if the supplier is in the scheme and if your dad gets Pension Credit, or he must apply if he is on some other benefits. (Elder care adviser)

There is such a lot to think about, and each idea needs someone to follow up a lead. It is not simple, and not much of it is about benefits from HM Government.

Age UK says that each year up to £3.5 billion of **Pension Credit and Housing Benefit** goes unclaimed by older people. They have an online benefits calculator that you can use to find out what benefits you are entitled to claim. A benefit calculator is an online form that you can fill in with your details, or those of the person you care for, which will work out for you what benefits you are probably entitled to. Another charity, **Turn2us**, is a national organisation providing practical help to people who are struggling financially. They also have a benefits calculator that takes less than ten minutes to complete and will tell you which means-tested benefits you may be entitled to, including tax credits. There is an A to Z of benefits on their website and a section called 'Grants Search' which can help you to look for funding organisations that might be able to give you a grant or other types of help.

Citizens Advice (which used to be called the Citizen's Advice Bureau) is there to give people knowledge and confidence. It is a national charity with a network of local charities that offer confidential advice online, over the phone and in person for free. You can find your nearest Citizen's Advice by entering your post code or town on their website. There you will also find a section on benefits which emphasises that it's important to make sure people get all the help that they're entitled to. There are pages and pages of information on benefits and tax credits if you're working or unemployed, sick, disabled, a parent, a young person, an older person or a veteran. There is also information about Council Tax and housing costs, National Insurance, payment of benefits and problems with benefits.

There is also a benefits calculator on the UK government gov.uk site, MoneySavingExpert.com and Step Change, the debt advice charity. All these are listed in Useful Contacts and Resources.

There is so much information which changes all the time that it is probably best to start with one of the benefit calculators. If you are not a British or Irish citizen there is a Support for Migrant Families tool you can use. This is for people who are not able to get benefits in the UK. Many sites also have an A to Z of benefits which is mainly useful if you know which specific benefit you are looking for, for example Cold Weather Payments or War Widow's Pension.

Chapter 4

Family dynamics

Unless you are an only child and the sole person with power of attorney, caring for an older relative involves negotiation, perhaps multiple negotiations, with other family members.

This book can't map out a path for you to decide the sharing of the responsibilities of caring, but it can help you to understand what some of the everyday challenges are and make suggestions for avoiding any pitfalls. You might be astonished to know how many common problems there are. When I write about these things in articles or talk about them to groups of carers, someone often comes back to me and says, 'It is as if you know my family!' Families are very different, but in some ways they are very similar. The differences are less important. The understanding of what it means to be in a family is the key issue. Sometimes it turns out that someone didn't even realise that they were part of a family.

Families come in all shapes and sizes

A family that consists of a mother, father and children who live together has often been presented as an ideal.

Once upon a time there were three bears – a mummy bear, a daddy bear and a baby bear and they all lived together in a house in the woods. (Traditional fairy tale)

Variations on this model family in the past have been condemned by religious, social and legal authorities as frankly unacceptable. Legal protection which is given to spouses, widows and children born within a marriage has been throughout history denied to those living outside this pattern. In some respects, and in some countries, it still is denied. The parents not being married or being of the same sex, or a single mother who was never married, might be treated as not just a variation but an abomination. Thank goodness families are now recognised to be a bit untidier. As divorce becomes simpler and less stigmatised, so stepfamilies are common. When parents remarry they create blended families and often share care between more than one household. Children may be raised by grandparents or other kin because their parents are not present as a result of death, illness or abandonment. It can be an economic necessity for parents to leave the child with other family members to bring in money for the whole family. The definition of a family is now extremely flexible. It includes partners who are child-free, whether same-sex or not and whether married or not. One of the more illustrative requests I've had was from a woman looking for advice for the care of her stepfather's stepmother.

The success of 'a family', whatever its shape and size, is based not on the structure but on the combined loyalty, support and, in the best cases, affection that can be drawn upon by all those involved. There is an expectation that they will help each other. This expectation is not always met, but it still exists. At times it is overwhelming. It might even prove impossible to fulfil.

In many places in this book familial relations are described in shorthand as if all the caring issues are between older parents and their sibling children. In reality the picture is much more intricate, involving grandparents, partners, nephews, great-aunts and uncles, cousins, stepchildren, cousins one and twice removed, step-grandparents, estranged family members, kinship carers, adopted family members and every variety of relationship in between, including in-laws and the parents of a former spouse (ex-in-laws?). It is often generational, with younger people supporting an older generation. That's not the only pattern, but it's one that this book focuses on because of the emphasis on caring for older people.

The key to this sort of relationship is that the people behave as a family even if they are not 'kin', that is, related by blood or marriage. Or civil partnership. Or living together. And that sometimes includes neighbours and friends who are so close that they are considered part of the family.

Women leading care but not decisions

There are significant numbers of men undertaking care and this book will be useful for men and women. But there is an important note about women. As a matter of fact, statistically most care is done by wives and daughters. Later in this chapter there is discussion about the fact that a woman often leads on the practicalities and yet struggles to be 'in charge' of decision-making. Reports from Age UK shine a light on women in families who are caring for loved ones. In 2021 they recognised that there are over a million 'sandwich carers' in the UK. These are people caring for an older relative as well as bringing up a family. Almost 70 per cent of them are women. Their ages range from twenties to sixties, but sandwich carers are most likely to be women aged 35 to 44. After the mid-forties the extent of childcare may reduce, but the responsibility for an older relative probably increases at the same time for those women.

In a report on women and caring, Age UK described the pressure on women:

The failings of the care system mean that women in particular are often left to pick up the pieces. Many are doing their best to provide care for their family but often at great personal cost ... Some are at breaking point and many more are at risk of it. They want and need to look after their loved ones, most wouldn't change that for the world, but they shouldn't have to do it alone and unsupported ... How much longer can women carry the burden of our crumbling social care system? ('Breaking Point – the social care burden on women', Care UK, 2019)

One reason why daughters often end up doing care is partly because of a traditional taboo that still exists in many societies. It may seem unacceptable that a son would give his mother a bath, but it seems entirely acceptable for a daughter to assist in this way. A daughter may even bathe her father. Intimate care in professional nursing or social care has often been seen as a female occupation. Although about 10 per cent of nurses are male, they tend to congregate in administrative and managerial roles and women are more focused on direct care roles such as care assistants or registered care staff.

As part of my research project, I did a survey of the older patients over the age of 75 about whether they preferred being cared for by a male or female nurse. They had quite firm views. Older people seemed to think that it was 'normal' for nurses to be female. The same survey discovered that the older women were uncomfortable about the idea of having any intimate care from a male nurse or care assistant. (Student nurse)

Whether it is family, a job or a profession, it is more likely that a woman will end up being a carer, either for cultural reasons or because statistically there are fewer men in the care workforce as nurses or care assistants.

Another issue is the relative earning capacity of men and women in any family in our society. When deciding who has to give up work to do care, it makes financial sense at that moment to choose the person who earns less. So again, the sacrifice is most often made by a female relative. But the financial benefit in the short term must be repaid by that woman in terms of loss of pension rights, professional seniority and income for the rest of her life.

Research indicates that the bulk of care typically falls on a single caregiver. It has been suggested that even when the majority of caregiving falls upon a woman, she may not be seen as critical to decision-making.

I am the oldest child and the only daughter, but my father is very traditional and he regards my brother as the head of the family after him. This tradition goes back as far as Roman law, so I'm not surprised we haven't changed it in my lifetime. Thus, when it came to discussing issues like whether he should have aids and adaptations in his house, it didn't matter what I said. It all came down to what my brother said should happen. Fortunately, I was able to persuade him to persuade my father to agree with what I was suggesting. My brother lives quite far away, and he could do this by phone. It was all I was asking of him and he did it willingly. He trusts me more than Dad does. But it's still annoying. (Daughter and carer of 98-year-old man living alone at home)

Daily, the daughter is probably most active in the decision-making processes about what is to happen. She may choose groceries and prepare his meals and organise shopping for clothes, shoes and household requirements. She may be dealing with bills, correspondence and doctor's appointments. She might even be undertaking housework and laundry. But when it comes to 'big' decisions, like whether to get a new fridge when the old one no longer works or new grab handles for the bath, it must be passed by her brother.

Who is involved in decisions?

Even those family members who don't take part in day-to-day care may still want to be involved in decision-making. It is usually better for the person cared for if everyone takes an interest. Things can go wrong, and if the lead carer is not coping and perhaps making unwise decisions, an extra person to help think things through might be helpful. Or it might be that they are seen as interfering.

It may be that other family members resent being excluded from decision-making processes. If the main carer decides that the time has come for her mother to go into a care home, her siblings might object to her coming to that conclusion and sabotage it. When feelings like jealousy or lack of trust are present, caregiving decisions can be undermined even if they are in the interest of the person cared for. Old people do not like being the cause of family conflict, and that doesn't always help in these circumstances.

Whether or not she agrees to having carers in the house depends on who she spoke to last. She told me she's quite happy with the idea, and then after she comes off the phone with my brother she has decided that it's not a good idea and she's not going to have it. It is infuriating because I have already contacted the agency and started to make arrangements. (Daughter, main carer)

The brother's feeling may be particularly strong if he is being asked to make a financial contribution to the cost of caring. He may discount the actual cost to his sister of providing all that care and think of it as somehow 'women's work', telling himself that she is happy and enjoys it. He would not see the point of spending real cash on care if it can be avoided. It might be that his self-interest extends to wanting to preserve his mother's resources, as he is a potential beneficiary of her will.

When making decisions about the care of an older person it would be disrespectful and inappropriate to fail to involve them, but their taking part depends on the level of their capacity. Sometimes the older person is in denial about the level of care that they need and the extent to which they are able to be independent. The person with most direct involvement is mostly likely to have a good understanding of what is needed. The difficulty sometimes is persuading other people of this.

As a carer you may find family members may be critical of your caring. But it's not just about family dynamics. Even neighbours have opinions and are happy to share them.

Ethel's daughter Pamela arranged for her to be moved out of the house that she had lived in for about fifty years to be near her in the village where Pamela lived. All Ethel's friends were furious. They felt it was too selfish of Pamela to take her away from the community that she knew. But Pamela was between a rock and a hard place. She had a job that meant she had to live 100 miles away, and commuting backwards and forwards even weekly to see her mother was grim for her. She could see that more intense care needs were coming, and she wanted to get Ethel settled before things got so bad that she would need her daughter every day. The friends and neighbours still talk about Pamela as if she is evil. (Family friend of Pamela and her husband)

It is just as well that Pamela lives 100 miles away. She has enough to do without having to endure the hostile looks of people who have never faced the sort of dilemma that Pamela had to resolve.

Why disagreements take place

The things that cause family conflict are as many and varied as families themselves. As we've seen above, even neighbours will pitch in and express views about the arrangements. If there is scarcity of resources for care arrangements, this is a source of discontent because difficult decisions must be made. Sizeable sacrifices are required from the family members which demand commitment, sometimes over a very long period. A crisis may bring old family conflicts back to light.

My sister was always bossy and interfering even when she was a teenager. Now that I am faced with having to do the daily care for our mother, it really annoys me the way she just swans in and starts telling me what should happen. (Older sister)

In this case the sisters are having to make difficult decisions and they have very little experience of joint decision-making. When one doesn't agree with the other, she puts it down to a personality defect that she remembers from decades before.

The Bible tells the famous story about the Prodigal Son. One son stays at home and tends the farm, and the other son goes away and is a wastrel. But when the traveller returns, the father kills the fatted calf in celebration. From time to time people mention this story and families tell me there is a parallel in their experience of providing care. The father forgives the returning child, no matter what. The Bible story doesn't really make it clear whether the brother is also forgiving when his sibling comes back.

I visit my dad every single day, shopping and cleaning for him, and my brother stays clear. But when Neil arrives once in a blue moon it is like Christmas and Dad doesn't stop talking about him for weeks.

*It's as if he doesn't even notice what I do for him. I am completely
overshadowed when 'Golden Balls' turns up and creates a circus for a
few hours. Neil's never offered once to help me. Dad may forgive him,
but I can't. (Gerard, brother of Neil)*

Jealousy may be an element of conflict. But in this case, there
is also a question of the disparate investment that the two sons
are making in their parent. The visiting son has little interest
in or commitment to the caregiving arrangements, and the
father appears to value his occasional entertaining contribution
over and above the commonplace tasks that the resident son is
undertaking.

Many families have a history where relatives have fallen out
after the death of a family member in a row over the deceased's
finances and estate. This is common in life and literature. The
grief after death resurrects a wide range of powerful emotions
such as jealousy and rivalry. There is a foreshadowing of this
turmoil in the anticipatory grief that people feel when an older
relative is becoming frail and ill. It is not just about money, even
though a potential legacy may be a major matter. Issues that have
bubbled under for decades come to the surface. Siblings who have
failed to start conversations about difficult questions during their
adult lives are thrown back to the feelings they had as children
as a starting point for awkward conversations now. Instinctive
responses cause reactions when there should be rational debate.

There is also a tension that arises from the different levels of
availability and what might be called generosity in the carers.
Anyone who lives in the local area is more available, especially if
they are retired or not in employment for some reason. It might
be suggested that they seem better able to fit caring into their
daily life. Other equally close relatives or friends might live further
away or be immersed in the world of work. As is explained in

Chapter One, it is still possible for someone who lives far away to make a major contribution to the care of someone, either financially or in terms of time spent writing letters or making phone calls.

My cousin is brilliant and selfless in the way she looks after Dad. She drops in every day with the newspaper and a few treats, like some fresh scones or a roll and sausage. On Sundays and holidays she gets him round to her house for a meal with the family, and on other days she'll bring over a bit of dinner. Not every day, because he likes to feel independent. I don't know what he'd be like if he did not have her nearby. I live in Canada so there's a limit to how I can help, but I send cash to pay for any bits of shopping she does for him. I never miss her birthday or those of her children. She says I make too much fuss, but I know she likes flowers and I make sure she has them often. He would never remember now, but I organise it so he 'remembers' her birthday and buys her a nice present now and again. I make sure to tell her all the time how much she is appreciated and show it in any way I can. (Daughter of Graham, 92)

They ought to be generous in providing support to the person who is giving the direct care at a local level, even if they can't come and help. And if they don't even try, the emotional depth of the response of others can be extraordinary. Families are torn apart by anger and resentment of carers who feel exploited by self-centred siblings who stood back while there was work to be done, then turned up in tears at the funeral and started making claims over any inherited property.

Anyone reading this who feels they are too far away to help with an older relative should get in touch with the main carer and just ask what they can do to help. You might be surprised at how easy it is to provide support. Don't be afraid to offer.

I told my brother that I was finding it hard and he asked what he could do. I just told him straight. To my astonishment he did it all, immediately. I don't know why I didn't ask him earlier, and he doesn't know why he didn't offer earlier. We were just not communicating. He didn't know the facts of what my daily caring is like. Now he does and it is great. We are working together. (Gerard, brother of Neil)

It may be that the facts are not at issue, but there is emotional history in the family that makes it difficult to agree. If one person has been trying to resolve the issue for a long time, feelings of resentment may have built up that are getting in the way. People take up positions which may give rise to negative behaviour. And even within a family, children have differing perspectives.

I'll do nothing for him. I don't feel any guilt about what my sisters do, running after him all the time. (George, son of Stanley)

It is not always obvious why siblings have differing views. You might suppose that George is inconsiderate or thinks caring is 'women's work'. But this story is not rooted in sexism. There is more behind it.

Stanley was a headmaster and was determined that I would excel. If I did not get the high marks he expected, he would thrash me with a cane. I will never forgive him for that and the fact that he treated my sisters only with kindness. They are always letting me know how much he needs their help now. If Stanley asked me for help now, I'd tell him to get lost. (George, son of Stanley)

There might even be differences in values. Some people believe that they 'pay forward' for the love and attention of their parents by loving and attending to their own children and passing the care down through the generations. They don't see the need to 'pay back'. Everyone is different – especially siblings.

Three kinds of decisions

In my experience of working with families, disagreements about how care should be managed or where care should be provided mainly seem to fall into two categories. First, it is very common that a decision must be made in a crisis. This can happen when an older person appears to have been living comfortably at home and then an incident takes place, such as a fall requiring hospital care. Once the person is in hospital the clinical staff start to wonder whether their patient will be able to survive by themselves at home. The clinical assessment and the social work assessment might lead to the authorities trying to persuade the person and their family that a placement in a care setting is needed. This can happen very quickly and under enormous pressure.

Then, second, there are considered decisions. How decisions are made in crisis circumstances is quite different from the way considered decisions are made over a time of discussion and reflection as the need for care becomes more evident over months and years.

There is a third sort of situation where no decision can be identified. In that situation stuff just happened. We will look at that also. It can be a situation that preceded a crisis. It might even be a contributory factor. It is almost as if nobody was prepared to make a decision. You might even say they decided not to decide.

In the following sections we will look at crisis decisions, considered decisions and times when decisions are being avoided.

Crisis decisions

Mum had a fall at home and was admitted to hospital. While she was in hospital she fell again and fractured her hip, so she was there for a long time. After they did a physio assessment, they decided that she probably couldn't go home safely because her toilet is upstairs in the

*house. We were under pressure to get her out of hospital and into a
care home as soon as possible. I had never been in a care home and had
no idea how you find one. (Daughter of Ethel, 92)*

In this situation, a rapid decision must be made about how to
deal with the announcement that Ethel cannot go home but
needs to leave the hospital. The rational thing would be to gather
evidence, consider alternatives and take time to agree the best
way forward. But there will be very many emotional elements
to the decision. The family may have promised that she should
never have to go to a care home. The mother herself may be
saying that she refuses to go and that she insists on going home.
How can the right decision be made under the circumstances?

Chapter Seven is about practical hints for carers, which
amounts to a big checklist of things that should be thought about
in anticipation of the things we know to be true about old age in
the UK. We know that the state and successive governments have
not supported carers but have relied upon them to provide care
for their families. So we should make plans for caring for ourselves and each other. We know what the common impairments
are in old age, and that many of them result in limited mobility and decrease in strength, so we should live in a house where
the toilet is accessible. We know that the commonest route into
care is via a hospital admission for a fall, so we should have at
least thought about home care, or what to do about a care home.
And if a care home is inevitable, which home, where and how it
would be paid for, hoping that the day would never come, but
at least having half an idea of what to do when it did. Especially
having had a clear discussion about what the older person prefers
and who would have the delegated 'difficult decision' power if
things suddenly went wrong and there was no time for a family
conference.

It is hard to make a rapid decision about what to do without having all the facts and information that are needed. Even if members of the family are deciding in a way that they think of as rational, it's still difficult for them to be completely objective in their choice. They will make the decision that is more satisfactory to them, even if their satisfaction is based on keeping the person they care for happy and safe. Sometimes safety and happiness are not evenly balanced in the equation.

I was asked to discuss the discharge plan with the two daughters, Anne and Betty, in respect of their mother who was our patient, Mrs Carr. For the older sister, Anne, the most important thing was to keep promises that had been made to Mrs Carr that she would never have to go into a care home. Betty was concerned that care at home would be more expensive, and Mrs Carr would run out of money before the end of life. I explained the relative costs of each. The care home would have been much less expensive in this case. Betty also thought there would be more company and activity and her mother would enjoy it because her previous idea of what a care home was like was just wrong. Anne suddenly said, 'You would say that because you want to hang on to the money' and her sister started to weep. I left them alone to talk to each other. (Elder care nurse)

The sisters were in an intense negotiation about what the right course of action would be but didn't have much time to think about it, because Mrs Carr was about to be discharged from hospital. It's necessary to recognise the importance of emotions at the core of any decision-making process. It would be a bad outcome if the two sisters fell out with each other. It's clear that their mother is near the end of her life and it's important that they still have a good relationship after she has gone. It's what she would have wanted.

Considered decisions

It is never too soon to think about what you want to happen when or if you become too old or frail to care for yourself completely independently. The discussion is hypothetical because you don't really know what the circumstances will be when the time comes for a decision to be made. However, you can assume that, financially, things are not going to be any easier for the government and the amount of state benefit is not going to increase radically, so some tough decisions will have to be made in the future.

In the light of that prediction, ideas to be explored might include decisions about whether to move to a different place, to move in with family, to save money or to spend now – a whole range of issues that will influence your own future and that of your family. This is something you should discuss with your family. If you suspect that, because of your age, relationship or sex, you are a person who is very likely to become a carer in your family, then you should start the conversation with the older person if they don't start it themselves.

My aunt was always practical and businesslike. We were very close. One day we were simply chatting. One of her oldest friends had gone to stay in a care home and I asked her what she thought of the home and whether she would ever want to stay in a place like that herself. I am glad that we had that conversation because when the day came, I knew exactly what she wanted me to do even though she wasn't in a position to tell me by then. (Jane, niece of Eleanor)

No one can guarantee that they are never going to need care, so no one can truly require of their children or younger relatives something too specific. However, many people do try to place this impossible burden on their family.

Mum said, 'I don't want to go in a care home. Promise you'll never do that to me.' I promised her that I will do my best when the day comes when such a decision has to be made. I can't say any more than that. (Daughter, 56)

There are things about ageing that can be done to delay the time when the need for care arises. There is more information in Chapter Two about how you can do that. Families should have these conversations with each other long before that need arises. If you're making a will, you will often find that the lawyer suggests granting a power of attorney at the same time. If you nominate someone to be your attorney, then you should have a conversation with them about what kind of decision they might have to make on your behalf one day and how you'd expect them to respond to the dilemmas that they may be presented with.

On my daughter's eighteenth birthday, the three of us went to see a solicitor and we granted powers of attorney for me and my husband to her on that day. There was a bit of a laugh about whether she could take over our affairs immediately, but we all knew because we had discussed it that this is a legal arrangement for a future emergency that we hope will never occur. (Mother, 42)

In Chapter Three there are more practical hints about how you can record advance decisions about what is to happen if a person loses capacity to make decisions.

There may be conversations that the family start to have without involving the person who will require care: negotiations about who would give up work, who would take the person into their own home, how the cost of caring would be shared between the children and any other issues that may not emerge but which are worth looking at. Then the children would be in a position to present options to the older person, allowing them to make a realistic choice.

There are those who are so determined not to be dependent that they would rather die. I do meet people frequently who are very afraid of being cared for, because they have heard such bad stories about old age and care and they have never experienced a loving, successful care relationship or witnessed a comfortable, happy care home or care-at-home lifestyle.

There's a woman in our village who told us she bought tablets off the internet that she can use if something like that happens. (Pub landlord)

There is little that can stop this woman killing herself if she is determined. At present it is not possible to ask for euthanasia in the UK, but proposals for legislation come up regularly. It would be an act of murder to administer a lethal medicine. Encouraging or assisting suicide or an attempt at suicide is a criminal offence with a maximum penalty of fourteen years' imprisonment. If the victim is discovered already unconscious, it is murder or man-slaughter to do something that causes the death of the victim. You must help to keep someone alive by calling for aid. The fact that she has bought the tablets, and is telling her neighbours about it, is a measure of how much this woman fears the future. I hope that the advice in this book will suggest that there is a better option than annihilation, and that comfortable and comforting care options will be more easily achieved if some thinking is done in advance. It would be a shame to have to shorten your life for want of some preparation.

No decisions

When people don't anticipate old age or discuss a range of possible plans they will end up looping back into crisis decision-making.

Talking about these things doesn't make them more likely or come sooner. Considering possibilities is not 'giving in' to ageing. It's more like insurance. We pay a lot for fire or accident insurance and most of us don't get anything back. We don't even want it back. We'd rather not have a fire or an accident.

Whenever I remember to take my umbrella, it never seems to rain. My plans for being dependent in old age are like that. I'm not scared, but I have the plan. I hope it never gets implemented. The only thing that would be scary would be having no plan. (Doris, 81)

How to resolve a family dispute

When they go low, we go high (Michelle Obama)

More and more families are consulting a caregiving expert or mediator. The increase in the number of older people needing care has given rise to a parallel increase in the number of family conflicts about decisions concerning care.

The worst possible outcome would be a family breakdown. That doesn't improve the family's capacity to provide care and may leave the main caregiver with an even greater emotional burden on top of their existing care responsibilities. And potentially it can leave the person who needs care in a vulnerable position: a family dispute is unlikely to be what they would have wanted either. But it is such a common problem that many people, including lawyers, faith leaders and dementia experts like me, who specialise in caring for older people, are frequently called on to provide mediation support in addition to providing advice on how to care. Other professionals in this field report the same increase in levels of need.

The person who needs care is at the centre. In the case of a person who is older and frail, there may be times when their family needs to decide on their behalf. Clearly, the ultimate responsibility lies with the person who has power of attorney (see Chapter Three). But even the attorney is required to consult with other relevant people in the family. When caring for someone who has reduced capacity to take part, for example in cases of dementia, it's important that they are involved as much as possible.

Whenever we had to make decisions about anything major Dad always used to say, 'I'll leave it up to you.' The mistake was to assume that meant he had consented. It was a wise move to discuss it with my brother, because Dad was capable of telling him that he didn't agree with it but had just gone along because I made him. My brother was able to confirm that we had come to an agreement. Sometimes it was too late to change back, like when I sold his car and he denied ever agreeing to that. (Daughter with power of attorney)

For this daughter, her brother was important as a witness to how decisions had been made, and his agreement was beneficial in giving her confidence that she was doing the right thing, even when their father changed his mind. Not every family member is so acquiescent.

When a family comes to me to ask about dementia, I am always prepared to talk about how they are coping and their feelings about their situation. I used to imagine that they would only want to know about caring, or the clinical details of the illness. Then I'd find myself refereeing a full-blown family dispute. There are limits to what anyone can do to help adult children reach mutually agreed decisions about how to best support their ageing parents and each other. My aim is to help them through a problem-solving conversation that allows them to work together with their shared mutual interest in the well-being of the person cared for.

When doing this mediation I am acting as a neutral facilitator between people to help them reach solutions to the issues that they disagree about. It's not my role to come down on one side or the other unless someone is proposing something dangerous or illegal. It's important to promote reconciliation within the family if they are in dispute. Mediation is different from negotiation. As a former trade union negotiator I know how to do that, but it's different. In a negotiation the different parties have opposing interests that conflict. That should not be the case in family discussions about caring for a loved one. It sometimes is, though.

David and Eleanor knew their mother, Grace, was not coping at home and she'd been diagnosed with a progressive condition that made it harder for her to be independent. Eleanor was starting to talk to Grace about care homes, but David kept putting Grace off the idea. At every opportunity he would present Grace with newspaper cuttings about care home scandals. He was trying to persuade Grace to come and live with him and his wife Jan. Eleanor didn't see what the benefit would be, as both Jan and David have business interests that keep them out of the house most of the time. As things stand, Eleanor was doing most of the care for Grace, including shopping, cooking and cleaning, and some personal care. Grace didn't want any strangers in the house and Eleanor was getting exhausted. David and Jan's children were about to go to university, and he had recently mortgaged his house to support his business. His aim was that Grace would sell her house and buy a half-share of his and move in to be looked after there. Eleanor is sure that the situation will break down and Grace will end up in a home anyway, but without any resource to pay for it. Grace is getting distressed and keeps changing her mind about what to do next. (Mediator summary)

David is motivated by his need for cash, and Eleanor doesn't believe his plan will help Grace. No alternative arrangement that involved Grace using her resources for herself would meet

David's needs. In these cases, there isn't really a role for a mediator. Her role is much more likely if there is already agreement and commitment to the care of the vulnerable person, and the only dispute is about how to best achieve that. It is to help the family reach their own solution. Of course, the mediator is seldom called in when the family situation is harmonious. Sometimes the situation gets so bad that it ends up in a court. But there can be a difficult passage even in cases where the family is normally a happy one.

Ludomir and Zofia, a married couple with children, needed advice on choosing a care home for Zofia's mother, Marzanna. Marzanna, a Polish woman who has Lewy body dementia, has two daughters. She was agitated and restless every night and during the day could not be left alone at home. Zofia had been telling her sister Wanda for months that the situation in the house was impossible. Marzanna was waking the household at hourly intervals in the night, going into the street and becoming lost. Wanda was very angry when it was suggested that Marzanna needed care-home care. When she phoned from Hong Kong, where she works in a bank, her mother always sounded fine to her. She thought that Zofia was going back on the agreement to care for her. Her idea of a care home in the UK was so dreadful, she thought it was cruel to 'put' their mother there. Zofia realised that Wanda could not understand how risky and stressful the position had become, and she found a way of explaining to her how the constant strain was affecting her marriage to Ludomir. Wanda had been concerned that Zofia expected her to pay for a care home, but I was able to advise that because Marzanna had few resources the local authority would pay, and if the family wished they could pay a top-up for extras. They were able to take Marzanna to a home they liked, which had Polish staff who could accommodate Marzanna's language, dietary, cultural and religious needs. Marzanna settled there very happily and was less lonely and agitated, and the two sisters are still supporting her in every way they can. During these discussions it became clear that Wanda was terrified of inheriting the disease which had caused Marzanna's illness, and that caused her to be in denial about the symptoms. (Dementia adviser)

In this case the sisters have been able to compromise and understand each other. They have reached an agreement. First they had to identify the issues and bring into the open what their interests were. Then they had to think about why they had taken a position and consider alternatives to the things that were causing concern. The issue of resources for the solution had to be taken into account. Apart from getting some information about how to pay for it, they worked out the situation themselves.

The situation is more difficult if one of the siblings is being unhelpful in their response.

My brother lives about 300 miles away and has very little contact with our mother. When he last did his annual visit, she pulled herself together and 'performed' very well for him. Most of the time she is crumpled and miserable and can hardly do anything for herself. I have been doing it all, before and after work. In the end I arranged for some help to come into her house for cleaning and cooking and asked him if he would like to make a financial contribution, but he would not hear of it. He asked how long it might go on for, so he could calculate if he could afford it. Which is a laugh because he is extremely well off. He managed to make me feel as if I was being lazy, as if it is my job as a daughter to do all this for her. He has always been miserly. I daren't say anything about him to her because he is the favourite. (Ruth, sister of David)

Although not much can change the sort of person David is or how he's perceived by his sister Ruth, the main thing is to get the right kind of care for the ageing parent. In Marzanna's case, the sisters managed to understand each other, and their shared commitment to finding what was best for Marzanna helped them come to an agreement. Their understanding of each other increased and they helped each other. Ruth, on the other hand, had great difficulty in getting David to agree to mediation, but he did in the end, if he could choose the mediator. The mediator, being professional, did not favour one view over the other. He didn't even work to improve the brother and sister's understanding of each other. Any increased mutual understanding by siblings is a possible benefit, but it's not the aim of the exercise. The cared-for person is at the centre of this. And relieving the physical, emotional or financial stress on the main carer is vital for that. No one can keep going when they are 'done in'. Through mediation it was finally agreed that Ruth would continue to provide care, but David would make a significant financial contribution that would relieve the burden for her, to an extent.

Everyone in a mediation must be capable of taking responsibility for decisions that are made and the outcomes. The responsibility for the outcome rests with the family, not the mediator. When I take part in this sort of conversation, I make it clear that I have expertise in caregiving, the conditions that the older person might have and care options such as care homes so that I can offer alternatives to contested solutions. If it works right, everyone wins.

Long-distance caring is a challenge for family dynamics. There are two sorts of long-distance carer: one is where you are the primary carer, and the other is where someone else is the primary carer and you are a friend or family member at long distance.

Mum was caring for Dad at home and we were doing all we could, but since we had moved to work 300 miles away there was a limit to what we could offer. (Only daughter, married)

If you are caring from a distance and there is a primary carer on the spot, there is a lot you can do. The vital thing is to ask them what they want and what they'd find useful.

My sister Elise lives near our mum in Glasgow and I'm living in New York. I remembered how much Mum liked to swim, so I suggested to Elise that she could take Mum to the leisure centre occasionally. Her response was to say that she'd pack the swimming things, and Mum, and all her medication on a plane and I could take her swimming in New York if I wanted to. (James, brother of Elise)

Clearly the idea was not appreciated. One can only imagine what Elise had been going through on that day when she responded so bitterly. She undoubtedly thought that James had a poor idea of what challenges she faced. If he believed that the problems presented by their mother could be fixed by a dip in the pool, he had another think coming. She wanted him to know this.

If Elise had been prepared for James and his possibly unhelpful or unrealistic suggestions, she might have responded by saying, 'Well, she doesn't need to go swimming right now, and that's not what I need. What would be much more useful would be …'. And she should tell James what she needs him to do. 'As I know you would like to help, here is something that you could do …'.

And if for any reason Elise and James are not communicating well and James is wondering what he could do, here are some ideas for him. All the following could be organised from the other side of the world.

- Phone calls at prearranged times, to entertain and engage the mother, taking some of the pressure off Elise and giving them something new to talk about.
- Facetime or Zoom calls to distract and allow two-way communication, letting James see how his mother has changed

as well as allowing her to see her son and anyone else he can get in on the call.

- The making of photobooks using images of places that his mother knows from the past which James could access on the internet. He could get the books printed and posted home for Elise to use to entertain her mother or leave with visitors to discuss.

- Compilations of family pictures or videos on disks that Elise could put on the DVD player to give her some respite while their mother watches it. Once you start compiling such things, it turns out to take a long time, and time is what Elise is short of.

- Making audio files of favourite music, or songs sung by family members, or even voices telling stories from the family history, which James could record for Elise to play for their mother.

- Post cards, greeting cards and letters, which are sometimes better than phone or video calls because the person can look at them again and again.

- Photographs to look at. So many of our images now are captured digitally and never make it on to paper. A physical picture can give hours of pleasure.

Another thing that can be easily organised is financial help. Carers spend their own money on what is needed for their loved one often without noticing. Then there are incidental expenses such as fuel and wear and tear on a vehicle, or other travel expenses. Time is money, and the unpaid carer puts in masses of hours. Other family members who are not available to care because they are in employment or living far away may be in a position to contribute financially. The most important thing for them is to ask.

For you as a carer, the key is to be ready with an answer. Know what you would ask for if anyone offered. And if they don't offer, ask them anyway. What have you to lose? And as the long-distance carer, you don't have to get permission to send thoughtful gifts or gift cards so the primary carer can buy themselves something they want.

Chapter 5

Your own health

The main part of this book has been about everyday things. It's been about working out what resources you as a carer might need to do your caring, getting those things organised, and practical stuff that needs to be sorted out by you. It has also included how you get help with your caring from other members of your family or friends and from private or public services. We've talked about the person you care for and shared ideas of how you can attend to the specific problems they might have and about getting help for them. But now it's time to talk about you, the carer.

There are two main things to think about here. One is how you are now, and what you are having to deal with in the present. Surviving the trials that keep coming up and keeping yourself well might seem like a big enough challenge on its own. But in addition to that, when you have enough energy — if you have enough energy — it is important to consider your own future.

How you are now

Carers often feel that they just need to get through the present day, or month, or year. Thinking about your own future might seem too much effort. I want you to believe that you deserve some time to think about it. It is the right thing to do, even if at this instant it seems like yet another burden you could do without. It is a good idea to consider what you are aiming for in advance, even if progress towards it is limited by what you are having to deal with right now.

Between the grandchildren and my dad, I don't have a minute to think. My head is buzzing. (Daughter of Graham, 93)

There is a discussion about what happens when you let go as a carer in Chapter Six. That's about a transition period. There are many transitions in caring. Sometimes you don't even realise they've happened until afterwards. The transition described in Chapter Six is much more about the time when you must get used to the person being in a care home or get through the stressful shift of handing over some of your care to others, such as home care workers or the staff in supported accommodation. You would still be caring in those circumstances even if you are doing a different kind of caring. Research shows that when carers spend time caring after that transition they focus on different aspects. As some of the mundane things like laundry and food are handled by the staff, there may be more time for social and recreational activities with your loved one. At night, you can sleep knowing that someone else is fielding the phone calls and taking care of midnight snacks, or trips to the toilet, or just the need for a chat in the hours before dawn.

This chapter is not about that, but about preparing for your own life after caring stops. First, it is about caring for yourself, and how to stay emotionally and physically healthy while being a carer so that you will be in fit shape to start afresh and enjoy your new phase of life when it comes. Because it will come, as long as you don't kill yourself in your work of caring. This can happen. Second, this chapter becomes more focused on how you prepare for the rest of your life after you have laid down your burden of caring for someone. It is all about caring for yourself and your own future. Many carers are not the sort of people who think about that. But you must.

Caring for yourself emotionally

The emotional aspects of care are very tiring, sometimes even more than the domestic chores and tasks.

I suggested to Mum she should get a home help and she said, 'Oh, no. I'm managing fine on my own without help!' She doesn't think of what I do for her as 'help'. My first thing when I reach her house once or twice a week is to bleach the toilet. Relationships are made more by what you don't say than what you do, so I bite my tongue, but my husband is sometimes furious. He's fed up being left alone at home while I tend to her. He says it is too much for me and my health is suffering and why doesn't the rest of the family do more? She's 150 miles away. Then the phone calls at night started. That's too much even for me. (Ana, daughter of Christine, 83)

Ana's husband is trying to be supportive, really. He thinks he's helping by pointing out that some aspects of the burden of care are unfair and affecting their time together. This idea of 'fairness' makes it emotional. It might be easier for Ana not to think of it as a question of being fair, but about doing what is practical. But that's not where he's at. Eventually, for Christine and her daughter, it will be time to start to think about professional help, but Christine is in denial. Regarding herself as a carer is the first step for Ana in taking on responsibility for a big decision like that, and it's not easy. But Christine doesn't even realise that she is now 'cared for'.

So many draining emotions are involved. Already in this example we've seen Ana's anxiety about her mother, her husband's irritation and even anger. There's her embarrassment about the housekeeping, and perhaps even disgust at the state of the toilet and guilt about only visiting once or twice a week. It would not be surprising if Ana also felt a lack of appreciation for the work that she does for her mother, along with tiredness and resentment. Ana's husband is feeling the loss of quiet time with his wife. And what is Christine feeling? Her strongest emotion is probably fear. She might be in denial, but that is because she is afraid of what is to come. Managing all these emotions is tiring, and you can be sure that Ana is not just experiencing her own emotions but managing everyone else's as well. She will be trying to make up for lost time with her husband and pacify him. She will be reassuring her mother. She's operating on reduced and interrupted sleep and she's about to have to make an expensive and unpopular decision. When I talk about this example to families someone always says, 'How come you know all about my life?' and they laugh, even though they're not happy about the situation.

You have to know that it is OK to be not OK and to seek help. The decisions that must be made by carers are tough, and you need to recognise this drive you have in yourself to make things better for everyone and acknowledge the effect that it has on your own physical and mental health.

I want to spend some time in my garden at last, and I want to be able to go to the cinema. I want to soak in a bath for an hour, with a book and out of reach of a telephone. It doesn't sound like a lot, but I've not been able to do that for about two years. (Daughter of Graham, 93)

Burnout

Burnout is a state of physical, emotional and mental exhaustion. The carer who is affected by burnout may start to have a changed attitude towards the person they are caring for. It's most likely to happen when you don't get the help that you need or if you're trying to do more than you're able to physically or financially. Sometimes people feel guilty for spending time on themselves rather than on their older relative or friend and so they stop essential self-care. The carer feels tired or stressed and may also experience anxiety and depression.

This breakdown is most likely to occur if you have difficulty in separating your role as a caregiver from your role in the relationship with the person. As a spouse you may feel that it is your job to keep them happy. As a child you may feel it is your duty to keep them comfortable and well. Your expectations may be unrealistic if you hope to have a positive effect on the health and happiness of the person involved and you are not getting any feedback to suggest you are having any success.

No matter what I do for Dad it doesn't seem to make any difference. He's always miserable. I turn myself inside out trying to please him, but he is still very low. I don't know what else to do. I am on my knees (Dan, son of Chima)

Depending on what it is that is affecting his father, Dan may feel frustrated that he is not able to make Chima feel better. But it may be that his aspiration is quite unrealistic. It may be that his father is someone who was never happy when others were looking after him and he has not changed. Even if Chima's main difficulty is a mental impairment, for example, like those caused by dementia, he may also be affected by depression. Being a carer for someone with depression is a very difficult task. You may never be able to release them from their feelings of desolation. Dan is placing an unreasonable demand on himself if he thinks he can cheer his father up. Depression is not about being cheerful. It's a fundamental physiological problem – a clinical condition. Of course, it is helped a lot by good company and support, but Dan can't fix it entirely through his own actions and behaviour and he risks harming himself by throwing too much energy into this hopeless task and feeling like a failure.

Everyone bears some responsibility to look after themselves. As a carer you still have this responsibility even if you've got into the habit of neglecting it. It is not OK to sacrifice yourself. It's illogical. The person you care for would not want it. If you neglect yourself while they still need care, you won't be able to help them.

Put on your own oxygen mask before assisting anyone else. (Universal airline safety message)

How can you take care of yourself? An important step is monitoring how you're feeling. You may need to try discussing it with someone else to be sure you're being realistic about whether or not you're able to cope with what is being thrown at you. Although it is possible that a family member might place unreasonable demands on the people who are caring for them, it might be that the caregiver is placing an unreasonable burden on themselves. A friend or other reliable third party could tell you if that's what you are doing. Many caregivers don't know when they're suffering from burnout and eventually get to the point where they cannot function properly, becoming ill themselves.

Burnout often looks like stress and depression. The person might start to be withdrawn from friends and family. They lose interest in activities they previously enjoyed, and they feel hopeless and helpless. When you're looking out for yourself, be mindful if you notice changes in your sleep patterns and your appetite, or if you find yourself getting ill more often. In extreme cases the carer might begin to feel that they could hurt themselves, or even the person for whom they are caring. This comes from complete emotional and physical exhaustion.

If you ever reach the point where you consider hurting your-self – stop. If the pain you're feeling has become unbearable, just talking to someone else can take some of that weight off your shoulders. It's incredibly sad that you feel so bad. You may feel that nobody cares about you, but there are people who will care for you if you allow them to. You have nothing to lose by giving someone else a chance to help. I care. I'm not with you at this moment, but these people are. Contact them now.

Supportline
Helpline: 01708 765200
Email: info@supportline.org.uk
www.supportline.org.uk/problems/suicide

Samaritans
Helpline: 116 123 (available 24 hours)
Text SHOUT to 85258
www.samaritans.org

If you reach the point where you feel like hurting the person you are caring for – stop.

The people who abuse those they care for are often found to be depressed and not getting enough support from other poten-tial caregivers or organisations. Sometimes the intensity of the illness or dementia of the older person causes burnout in the carer. The carer may have resorted to alcohol or other substances to cope with their own stress, and that is affecting their thinking and self-control. Both the abuser and the person being abused are suffering. If you are in a relationship of trust with an older relative or friend you care for and you fear you are causing harm or distress to them, get in touch with someone immediately and ask for help. You might start with your GP, faith leader or a family member. Professional counselling would help if you can

access it. Elder abuse is when a person in a relationship of trust
causes harm or distress to an older person. It can be a single or
repeated act, or it can be a failure to act. If you suspect that an
older person in need of care is being abused, contact Hourglass
(formerly known as Action on Elder Abuse) on 0800 808 8141 for
advice on your next step. Their website is listed in Useful Contacts and Resources.

Your mental health

It's essential for anyone's mental health to have someone they
trust who they can talk to about their feelings. For a carer, this
could be a friend or a neighbour or someone you meet through
one of the support organisations for carers. You will find contact
details for those organisations in the Useful Contacts and
Resources chapter.

It's important that you set realistic goals for yourself, accept
that you will need help and make sure you ask others for that
help. It might be that there is a local carers' voluntary organisation, or you may be able to get help from the local authority.
If you have a faith it could be that, through your place of
worship, you will find friends you're happy to talk to and who
can provide advice, information or practical help. Many faith
leaders are trained to support people dealing with a wide range
of physical and emotional issues. You have to recognise your
own limits and be honest when the time has come to speak to
someone else.

The more you understand about the disease or condition that
your loved one is suffering, the more you will be able to predict
what is coming and it will be less of a shock when it happens. If
you know what the progress of the illness is, usually you will be
aware that a time may come when the person needs to be helped

outside the family home or in a residential facility. The more you know about the illness, the more effective you will be in caring for the person.

Physical health

Your physical health is vital for maintaining your mental health. People often talk about these two things as if they were separate, but they are closely intertwined. The basics are sleep, eating, physical activity, sunlight and being careful around medicines (or drugs) and alcohol.

Sleep

Sleep is vital for your physical and mental health. It isn't just the length of time that you are asleep, although on average eight hours is recommended for most people. The quality of your sleep affects how much your sleep is helping you. If it is constantly interrupted or if you're unable to settle because you're listening carefully for someone else who might need you in the night, you're unable to go into the deep levels of sleep that your brain requires to repair itself after a long day. So you need to be sleeping in a dark room, without being disturbed by noise.

I was never able to sleep at night because I had to keep one ear open for my son getting up to go to the toilet. I was afraid that he might fall down the stairs. Then the social worker got me a passive infrared beam, which is a little light that goes beside his bed. When he gets out of bed and breaks the beam a buzzer goes off under my pillow and wakes me up so that I can go and help him, or at least lie in bed and listen until I hear him getting back into his bed. The change was amazing. I slept more deeply knowing that I would be wakened if I was needed. And curiously, the number of times that he was getting up during the night was drastically reduced. It is almost as if our anxiety was keeping both of us awake. (Mother of Jeff, who has working-age dementia)

This small, inexpensive item of technology has transformed the sleep and daytime alertness of both the person cared for and the carer. The importance of sleep is often discussed in newspaper and magazine articles and on the internet, and there is extensive advice about how to get good-quality sleep. There are some great books on this and there is helpful advice on the NHS website https://www.nhs.uk/live-well/sleep-and-tiredness/how-to-get-to-sleep/

There is more about sleep in the Big List in Chapter Seven. Remember the concept of 'sleep hygiene', which is about preparing your room and yourself for rest.

Eating well

A balanced diet is one that will keep you strong and energetic enough to provide care. You probably already know what a balanced diet looks like. The problem is fitting that into your busy day. If you are stressed you may not feel like eating at all. If you are busy you may end up eating too many of the same kinds of food. No food is wrong. It's the balance that matters.

I don't have the time or the energy to prepare meals for myself and when I have prepared something for Mum, I don't feel like eating the same thing. I never sit down to eat and I have put on weight. When I feel hungry, I just head for the biscuit tin. Sometimes even when I don't feel hungry. (Ruth)

If you are worried about weight gain, there are very many places where you can go for advice and you don't need me to write all that down here. Attending a class is great and there are some that are online, but the problem is usually about where you are going to get the time. It might be an occasion to make time for yourself by asking a friend to cover for you.

There is one thing that is definitely worth repeating. The key recommendation in nutrition books and programmes is about planning. If you don't have the biscuits in the house, then you can't eat them. And when you are doing your shopping, having a plan makes sure that you stock up on the sorts of things that you think you would be better off eating, like fruit and vegetables and healthy snacks. Don't forget to drink lots of water. Sometimes when we are thirsty we mistake that for hunger, and water is good for you.

Unhealthy snack foods are often inexpensive, and they've been designed to be attractive and easy to consume. Many carers have problems balancing their budget because of the cost of caring and the way it prevents them from taking paid work. This makes it difficult to buy the sort of food that would be better for you. When you are caring it is important to make sure you are getting all the financial help you are entitled to so you can afford to buy the things you need for your own health. There is more about accessing Carer Allowance in Chapter Three. It's complicated, but the Carers Trust and other organisations have benefit calculators to help you. There is also the Carers UK advice line (details at the end of the book in Useful Contact and Resources).

I started to do my supermarket shopping online during Covid. I haven't stopped because it lets me take my time choosing what I want according to the meal plans that I've made for myself. I can pick up bargains and 'own brands' and I'm less likely to be tempted by things that I see on the shelf. It's quite nice having someone deliver it to the door as well. That saves time and energy. (Ruth)

Get things delivered. Delivery charges may be offset by fewer impulse buys, and having time to plan meals for an online shop might help you get the best possible nutrition for yourself.

Physical activity

A healthy weight is not the only marker of good physical health. As we get older it's important to maintain muscle strength. If you fall on the floor, you want to be able to get up again. Eating protein is important for your muscles, but you must also exercise. If you're a carer you're perhaps not going to have time to go to the gym, so it's useful to know of simple exercises that you can do at home to improve your muscle strength.

Everyone should do some type of physical activity every day. Any activity is good for you, and the more you do, the better. You don't have to go to the gym to strengthen your muscles, but a gym can be a great place to meet people or even have time to yourself. Some activities such as yoga, Pilates and tai chi have value in relieving stress and tension as well as improving muscle strength. You could join a class, but if your caring responsibilities make that difficult there are videos and books that would help you work out on your own at home.

Some daily activities, such as carrying heavy shopping bags or energetic shovelling and digging in the garden, count as muscle-strengthening exercise. To get benefit from them do these things to the point where you need a short rest before repeating the activity. You will find exercise routines and workout videos for beginners on the NHS website at www.nhs.uk/conditions/nhs-fitness-studio/

You should aim to do up to two or three hours a week of moderate exercise. That would include brisk walking, riding a bike or pushing a lawnmower. Light activity is anything you do by moving about. Housework and pottering around your home would count. The good thing about light exercise is that you are not sitting or lying down. Being still is now thought of as presenting the same health risk as smoking. So try to keep moving.

Before doing any vigorous exercise you need to check with your doctor if you have any medical conditions. Of all the equipment you can buy the most important is comfortable, properly fitting shoes. These would help anyone to get up and walk. Try to spread your activity over the week. This seems to work better than just doing one or two days of intensive exercise and then sitting down for the rest of the time.

Sunlight

For those reading this book in the UK, the notion of getting out into the sunlight might seem like a wishful one. But for the purpose of your health any daylight is good. People in the UK suffer from vitamin D deficiency as a result of not exposing their skin to the daylight enough. Vitamin D is vital for your bone health. Getting out in daylight is not just about the sun's rays, it's also about getting some fresh air and exercise. Taking a walk outdoors is good for your health and can make you feel better. Activity reduces stress, and if you can go outside and do something you enjoy then that will help both your physical health and your mental health.

Taking a dog for a walk is not only good for the dog but allows me to meet and chat with other dog walkers. I can't have a dog of my own because I've got too much to do, but I've joined the local 'borrow my dog' website and they are really delighted if you will take their dog out now and again. I have my favourite pups! It really cheers me up to get out and about for an hour with a wee pal. (Glenys)

Don't forget to ask other people for help with getting out. It may be that a friend is able to stay in with the person that you're caring for to allow you to get up and go.

Alcohol and drugs

Not much attention has been paid to the relationship between carer burden and the use of alcohol. Health and social service professionals now recognise that carers who experience social and emotional burdens are at risk of using alcohol to alleviate the stress that goes with caregiving. Using alcohol is a poor coping strategy for multiple reasons. Depending on the amount of alcohol taken, there is a risk both to yourself and the person you are caring for. Research has indicated that female dementia carers are more likely to use alcohol than other women of the same age. Increased use of alcohol is more common in people who don't have much social support. It has been suggested that carers who have a high level of emotional burden will drink more than others.

If it is the case that your drinking has become a problem, you can get help. One thing that will really make a difference is if some of the duties that you have as a carer are taken from you. Other family members or friends may be able to help while you seek treatment. **Respite care** is vital. People think of respite as being 'for the person cared for', but it is for the people doing the caring. It is great if you can access it and there is advice about how to do that and more about how to ask for help from family and friends in Chapter Seven, but the most important first step is for you to seek help about alcohol. You should talk to your GP, and they will be able to tell you what extent your drinking is affecting your health and give you information about local support programmes.

Some carers may misuse medicines like benzodiazepines or use prescription drugs to treat the various mental strains associated with the anxiety and loneliness of the caring role when they have been putting someone else's needs above their own. If you are a carer in need, there are resources available that can help you and the person you are caring for. Your doctor may prescribe you medicine for depression or pain safely if you're able to take them as prescribed. But the chances of abusing them are higher if you are a carer. If your use of alcohol or medicines is starting to reduce your capacity to care for yourself and your loved one, then you need to look for help. As a carer it is sometimes difficult to accept that you need help because you feel you are expected to be resilient and take everything in your stride while caring for others. But you must reverse that role to get the help that you need.

Loneliness, social exclusion and personal relationships

When I was in the depths of despair, my judgement was clouded by loneliness. I thought that everyone was too busy for me and that they had their own problems to deal with. So I didn't reach out to them. Instead I would binge-watch Netflix, and the following day I couldn't even remember what movies I had seen. (Antonia)

Research has shown that people who are carers suffer from loss of their social and family lives because of their caring duties. Daughters were the most likely to report deleterious effects on their lives, but everyone is different. One person might enjoy or even crave solitude whereas another might find that it makes them despondent. It is sad to feel a lack of sympathetic companionship. Loneliness is the individual response to this situation.

As a carer you may feel isolated even when there are lots of people coming in and out of the house. No matter how friendly the care workers are, they are not what you're looking for. There may be one or two key people who you really want to have contact with. You are already busy, but this is another job that you have to take responsibility for. You must reach out to people and tell them that you are thinking about them and that you miss them. They might even be holding back because they think you have no time for them and you don't need them.

A study by Age UK found that almost half of carers reported that romantic relationships are damaged by their caring responsibilities, and more than a third are uncomfortable talking to friends about their caring duties. Not having free time, being short of cash, being tired and unwell ... all of these make it more likely that you will not want to make the effort of keeping up with others. You may decide to join a carers' group where there are other people going through the same experience as you. Or you might want to reconnect with old friends and acquaintances and open up your horizons.

On days when I am lonely and I can't bring myself to go out of the house I open my drawer of postcards and stamps and get my address book. I send a postcard to lots of people and make sure my address and phone number are on there and tell them that it would be great to be in touch. Not many people send snail mail these days. I get a surprising number of interesting replies and when they come through the letter box it is a nice treat on the days when they arrive. (Janet)

Janet has made a plan for when she is lonely to use the time well. The investment she makes at that time brings her more company and joy later. Reaching out and sending mail to people brings pleasure to them as well. As a carer, you already know what personal satisfaction you give to people by caring for them with a touch like this. You don't even need a message. Just say, 'I saw this and thought of you.' This was a phrase used by Royal Mail in the past when they were trying to encourage people to use the post more. It is very clever because it really works to keep people in touch.

Getting professional help

GPs are becoming much better at identifying carers and your role should be recorded on your medical record. The carer registration form entitles you to a variety of benefits including free flu vaccinations. You should tell your GP that you are a carer to make sure that you are registered. Your local surgery may offer other benefits. During the recent pandemic, arrangements were made to ensure that carers were vaccinated. Without those carers very many more vulnerable people would have had to go to hospital, and hospitals were already under terrible pressure. The relationship you have with the GP should be like a partnership.

The health centre might also offer flexibility with appointment times, both for yourself and for the person you are caring for.

The appointment system for my GP is dreadful. For a routine appointment you have to phone up at 8.30 in the morning when the lines are jammed with people trying to get through. The last time I tried I used the 'call again' function on my phone and that meant I only had to keep tapping one button. I dialled 148 times between 8.30 and 8.45 before I got through. (Juanita)

If the health centre knows that you are a carer, you may be exempted from that frustrating and time-consuming morning competition. You need to make an arrangement and agreement to share information about the condition of the person you are caring for, with their consent. You can also find out if you are eligible for one of the free NHS health checks. Doctors know that caring can negatively affect your health in ways that include depression, stress, high blood pressure or back pain.

GPs also know that sometimes the health problems only show up after the person that is cared for has died or gone into a care home. Somehow the carer manages to keep putting one foot in front of the other until their job is done, and that is when their health collapses. At the health centre you may be able to get information about Disability Living Allowance or Attendance Allowance. At the very least they will be able to put you in touch with organisations who can help such as Care UK. There is more about allowances in Chapter Three, but a local organisation with local information or a national organisation with an up-to-date website is the most reliable source of information because the situation changes frequently.

In summary, all the physical things that you can do to improve your health such as exercise, sleep and nutrition will also help you with your mental health. Managing stress is an issue on its own. It can be hugely helped by activity and exercise and doing something that you enjoy. If you're able to follow the advice about connecting with others and being sociable, then you may find that this helps you to get back into things you used to do, like going to the cinema or taking part in a club. Many of us who are carers truly enjoy doing things for others, but for our own mental health it is crucial to do things for ourselves. This means you must ask for help whenever it is needed. And recognise that you don't always spot when it really *is* needed.

Finding replacement care to allow you to fulfil your own needs is covered in Chapter Seven under the 'Big List'.

Your future after caring

While you are caring you must not forget that there may come a time when you yourself need care. It is important to think ahead about how you're going to live after the person you care for is gone. It is not just about the freedom to do things that you have always wanted to do. You need to think about where you're going to live and how you are going to manage financially or get work.

Eleanor went back to live with her mother Gladys after she graduated from university. Gladys had very poor health, and although Eleanor went away to work from time to time in other cities, there was always some emergency that brought her back home. Eleanor didn't work in the last ten years before Gladys died. They were very fond of each other and had a nice life together. But at the age of 45 Eleanor was left with no career and no means of support. In addition, the private tenancy for their flat was in her mother's name, so Eleanor was made homeless. (Social work report)

Being a carer can involve a significant amount of self-sacrifice, but you need to think ahead about how you're going to support yourself after your caring role has ceased.

Working-age carers and finance

Eleanor may have been able to find an employer who was operating a 'carer-friendly' workplace that would have allowed her to work alongside her caring duties. If you are employed, you may discover that your employer has a policy about supporting carers in the workplace. You could bring to their attention the publication from the CIPD (Chartered Institute of Personnel and Development) which is a guide to providing support for people (more details in Useful Contacts and Resources). It recognises that carers keep families together and contribute to society including saving the economy a lot of money. The definition of a working carer is someone whose caring responsibilities have an impact on their working life.

From a legal point of view, employers have obligations under flexible working regulations and equality legislation relating to disability which could apply to carers who work for them. Employers cannot treat carers less favourably than other people who do not have caring responsibilities. The Equality Act 2010 protects a person who experiences discrimination because they are associated with someone who has a disability. Carers also have the right to take unpaid time off work for dependants in an emergency. From a moral perspective it's the right thing to do, but it also enhances the reputation of a company if it is good to carers.

Workplaces are supposed to have a clear definition of what it means to be a carer. Some create a carers' register. Formal policies and procedures make life easier for both managers and carers when faced with the need for special arrangements, flexible working options, career breaks, access to well-being sessions and carers' support networks.

In our organisation we have a mix of solutions that we can use such as flexible working combined with time off or special leave. All managers are trained to understand what caring responsibilities might be. We also have sources of information that people can access through the HR department. They are advertised on posters around the workplace. (Human resources adviser)

Even though there are new initiatives around this, it is clear that many carers lose traction in the workforce if they are unable to work because of caring duties. The International Longevity Centre undertook a report in June 2021 which spoke of people in Generation X (those born between 1965 and 1980).

The future financial well-being of many of the 1.7 million Gen Xers who are carers is being severely hampered as caring responsibilities can limit their ability to work and in turn save, while also contributing to poorer health compared to non-carers. (https://ilcuk.org.uk/1-7-million-gen-x-carers-risk-retirement-poverty/)

The research highlights that many carers are too overwhelmed by other priorities to think about retirement plans. This is particularly true for those who are caring for both children and an adult, that is, sandwich carers. The report recommends extending existing legislation about parental leave to make available statutory paid leave for carers. Increased flexibility of rules in the workplace is needed because the demand for informal carers is going to rise rapidly to meet the needs of the ageing population. Flexibility was achieved very quickly for many jobs during the COVID-19 pandemic, and so it's really important that this is addressed for the ageing population. You wouldn't call global ageing a pandemic, but it's a health issue that requires urgent attention.

Flexibility in working hours is vital for young grandparents. There are 1.5 million grandparents in the UK under the age of 55, and many of the working-age grandmothers are providing childcare for grandchildren in addition to caring for adult children who still live at home and supporting their own ageing parents. It may be difficult to find jobs offering flexible hours, and so the younger working grandmother may drop her job to help the family. Campaigners are pressing for more flexible options.

But until that utopia is built, what can you do?

Chapter Three has more details about finance. It includes advice about what to do if you are caring and you are struggling with living costs. It would not be surprising. A huge number of carers become impoverished as a result of their caring duties. It is vital to do this while you are caring with a view to the future. If, at the end of your time as a carer, you find that you have not only built up levels of debt but have been left in a position where your capacity to earn is reduced, it is too late to act. That chapter tells you more about how to find out about Housing Benefit, tax credits, Pension Credit, Income Support, help with Council Tax and even using a food bank. If you get all the benefits you are entitled to while you are caring, then you make things better for yourself later. You must take the long view and take up anything you can.

Your own future care needs

People sometimes joke about their future needs. If you are thinking about yourself in advance and exploring some ideas about your future, you are doing the right thing. Not enough people think about this early enough or have the conversations that are needed with their family. The addresses in Useful Contacts and Resources include organisations that can help you with your decision-making. Thinking about the possibility of dependence doesn't mean you are more likely to have to rely on someone else, but if that day comes your decisions will have been properly thought through and you'll be making the best of things. It might never happen, but the possibility is there. It is easier for you to sort some things out now rather than leave them to those coming behind and to your future self. This is especially true, because dependence on others sometimes occurs suddenly. A fall or sudden illness could lead to a hospital admission, after which you might not be well enough to go on independently and without some form of care.

Mum always says that if she reaches the stage that she needs help, she wants us to shoot her. She asks me to promise that I'll never let her go in a care home or have strangers in the house to care for her. I tell her I'll put her in a sack and leave her down by the harbour for someone to collect. To be honest, I have no idea what we will do if that day comes when she can't be independent. (Daughter)

The mother in this case has probably been amazing all her life and cared well for her parents as well as her children, but by not making feasible suggestions about what should happen if she can't manage in future, she's missing out or failing in one aspect of being the head of a family. It is part of caring for your children to have that discussion with them about what might happen if you are lucky enough to grow sufficiently old to be frail. You need to lead the discussion about how you are all going to manage that together. You may need their help then, but you can help now by doing as much as you can in advance. This can be as simple as getting a power of attorney set up, decluttering your possessions and getting your papers in order. If you don't do it they might have to, and why would you leave them with that hassle?

For years Mum used to say when we visited her house that there was a drawer in the dresser, the bottom drawer, that had all the papers in it. I didn't want to look. I didn't even want to know. But when she got dementia, I found files and folders with details of her bank accounts, pensions and insurances, utilities, lists of people she'd like to be in touch with and even notes of which of her little treasures like rings and bracelets that she wanted the grandchildren to have. (Son)

It is clear from talking to hundreds of older people and their families that many of us have a dread of losing independence. Our idea of what a care home is like may be shaped by the bad stories in the news. The COVID-19 pandemic made people justifiably afraid of care homes, because so many residents died there even though they were kept in isolation from their families to try to protect them from the virus. It is true to say that many will have died from loneliness. But it would have been impossible for all of them to go back to their families or live alone. It is encouraging that after the initial pandemic year, the public perception of care homes improved, in recognition of the heroic work of front-line staff there.

I have a positive view of care homes, having had experience of working with a great number of good ones. Many of the fears that people have are unfounded. It might be that a care home is the best solution to the caring challenge, even if it was not the first choice. You can live there in comfort knowing that, in addition to any friends or family, there are new people around who will care for you and care about you. Life's daily worries will be taken care of. It can be a time to relax and enjoy yourself.

It's like being a student again. When I went up to university over seventy years ago, I had a room of my own for the first time in my life. A cleaner changed the sheets and did some dusting once a week. I filled the shelves with books and got myself a record player and I could read and listen to music to my heart's content, and then go to talk to other people if I felt like it and eat in the student refectory. I used to think they were the happiest days of my life. But here I am again in my own room. Not a lot of space for books or records, but now I've got an Alexa, and my Kindle with large print, and I can talk to people on my iPad. And my own shower room. I'm maybe in God's waiting room, but this is a little bit of heaven already. I'm so happy here. (Retired professor, 92)

This professor has decided for herself. But if a person has lost their capacity, someone else must make decisions about care. Statistically, the one who does this for a parent is likely to be an oldest daughter, as has been shown throughout this book. Sometimes it is a group of siblings. Sometimes they fall out (see Chapter Four). Whoever has been caring for the person at home may have to make the decision that the time has come for a residential care solution. The most important thing is to have discussed it with the older person in advance. Knowing their previously expressed wishes helps the main carer deal with all the people they may have to convince or persuade. Being clear about it in advance with your friends and family is massively helpful, even if they don't want to think about it at the time.

I've talked this through with my daughter. I told her I want to stay independent for as long as possible, but a day might come when I don't realise that I need to go in a home. No matter what I'm saying then, I want her to see to it and find a nice one. If I've got dementia or something and I don't even know who she is I don't even want her to visit me, unless she really feels she has to, for her own sake. Just as long as she checks up that everything is OK. I've been saying this to her since she was a teenager. She got power of attorney then and it's all sorted, and I know how it'll be paid for. (Eleanor, 56, in great good health)

If you talk to Eleanor's daughter, she'll tell you that it was hard when her mother started these conversations. As an only child, she really didn't want to contemplate the day when she'd have to say goodbye to her parents for the last time. To begin with, it made her cry to think of it. But it's part of growing up. It's part of life.

Some children are not so lucky.

My mother always said that she would never want to go into a nursing home. She got ill and frail in her eighty-ninth year and after some months in hospital my partner and I brought her home to my house. After thirteen weeks of sleepless nights, I couldn't go on any more. I had to tell her that we were moving her to a nursing home. I'll never forget the turn of her head when she looked away from me. (Anders)

Anders made a very hard decision, after trying his best to do what his mother had always said she wanted. Those of us who have children who love us are very lucky. The least we can do for them is to tell them that if they ever must make such a hard decision, you trust them to make the right one. Give them the blessing that, even if you don't fancy the idea currently, you accept that when the time comes they will have done their best for you, and by that stage it is better for them and best for you to make a move into residential care. It is never too soon to tell them this. Tell them even if you are 40 and they are 20 years old. If you are 90 it is still not too late. Even if it's not the most attractive idea in prospect, you might be surprised to find that it is comfortable and even fun. But from the day you tell them until the day you die, or move into a care home, whichever comes first, you can have the comfort that you protected them from that unnecessary pressure and from a sense of guilt that can tarnish their memory of your later years.

I've decided not to put a burden like that on our children. I've said I wouldn't want a care home if it's practical to avoid it, but things can happen to change how independent I am and I'd rather be in a home than be a burden to them. I don't want them to carry the burden that my mother placed on me. I did my best for her, but it's like she never forgave me for not being able to cope. I've 'forgiven' my lot in advance and given them my blessing. Anyway, it might never come to that. (Anders)

Chapter 6

Change and letting go

In this chapter we look at major changes in your caring relationship. This can happen when you are forced by circumstances to give up caring for someone. The reason might be related to your own health or circumstances. You may choose to stop providing care. This change of relationship can be when the person moves in to be looked after in a care home. In the end, your life changes completely when the person dies. It is not unusual for someone to feel depressed with any of this, especially if they are already exhausted from caring. If you feel like that you could try talking to someone you trust. Your GP may understand and be able to put you in touch with help. Remember that the Samaritans are there for anyone on 116 123. Don't try to manage this alone.

On the other hand, some people feel liberated and rush into a lot of new activity, making up for lost time. That might be fun. But it could be that taking some time to consider what you want to do would be good. You may not have had much time to think about yourself for a while.

This chapter looks at all three of these potential changes in your caring role – changing and stopping providing care yourself, helping the older person go into a care setting, and the end of their life.

Changing your role as a carer

I used to visit my widowed uncle every single week, take him out for lunch and fill up his fridge and cupboards with all the food that he needed till my next visit. It was quite a long journey to get to him, and it took a full day going back and forth. Then I was unwell myself and for about two months I was unable to visit him. Until then I had no idea how much I was driving myself into the ground and I was embarrassed to confess to others that it came as quite a relief to be able to say I was unable to drive. I just couldn't do that support any more. (Alastair, nephew of Adrian, 86)

For Alastair the first change was that he had to give up his caring role because he was ill for a couple of months. He was ashamed that he found it such a relief not to have to continue doing what he had undertaken to do. However, he later found it disconcerting when other people took up the reins and replaced him very quickly.

Imagine my surprise when other people appeared out of the woodwork and started doing things for Adrian. My cousin even started to take him to the shops and got him to do his own shopping. It turned out that he was able to take himself down to a café for cooked meals whenever he felt like it. I was annoyed with him for not making a bigger effort before and I was sort of jealous of my cousin. Why had he not helped earlier? Also, bizarrely, I found myself feeling that my cousin was trying to replace me in my uncle's affection. I know it doesn't make any sense. But I felt bad. I thought I was essential, and I was so very quickly replaced. (Alastair)

Alastair has quite a mixture of emotions! It's a combination of relief, anger, jealousy and confusion. But in the end he made a conscious decision to step back from his previous, more intense caring role. He is different from Miriam.

Miriam made sure that everything was taken care of when she was not with her mother. She did laundry, made meals and cleaned. When work meant she had to travel away, she would organise cover for her mother's care, arranging for neighbours and friends to take her place. When on business trips she found it hard to focus and would be constantly on the phone to her mother and the friends, checking that things were OK. Her own teenage children would complain during these trips because their father would make them do things for themselves. Normally Miriam did everything at home for them, but she was getting angry and irritable and snapping at them all, including her husband. (Dementia care adviser)

Miriam is exhausted. Eventually she will become unable to look after anyone because she is doing too much for everyone and she has failed to take care of herself. Unlike Alastair, she has not yet had an illness that made her stop and take stock. Caring for others is causing her stress, but she feels that she has to keep doing it. She is carrying her mother, and her children, as well as work. She never even stops to ask herself why. It is time for a change, even though she doesn't realise that yet. She might want to examine the unmet need that her family has. Her husband needs her support to encourage the children to grow up and be more independent. For that she should care for herself more and keep an eye on those under her own roof. Doing things for people has become like an addiction: she continues to do it even though it may harm her.

As a carer you must set some boundaries. Your role nourishing others should leave room for you to focus on your own future. That sometimes means stepping back.

My dad always says, 'You don't need to do that for me.' And I do it anyway because I think he needs it. One day I decided to take him at face value. I was almost as surprised as he was at the change.

If he said not to do it, I didn't. It is possible that previously I was robbing him of his independence. Either that or I was denying him the opportunity to see his own limitations. He thought he could do it and he was never proved wrong. He didn't know he needed help because I always did everything. Eventually, after I stopped, he accepted the reality and decided to move out of his enormous empty house into sheltered accommodation and hire some help. Both our lives improved. I think it is easier to love each other again now. (Angela, daughter of Henry, 94)

Henry was having a problem accepting his ageing and frailty. Because Angela was taking the problem away from him, she was not allowing him to grow in understanding. She may have enjoyed having him dependent on her to begin with and happily took over his needs entirely. They were colluding. But then she realised that she could not keep it up and it wasn't helping him in the right way.

Another example of what might be called 'over-caring' is when the carer's concern for their ageing parent leads to lots of arguments about how best to do it. The older person becomes aware of the tension in the family, and this makes the parent feel as if they are a burden to everyone. And the carer does not even notice what is happening until they become ill.

What is the answer? Everyone is different, but here are some ideas if you find you are over-caring for an older relative:

- Learn to say no. Love saying no. Embrace it. (And get used to it.) That means setting boundaries and sticking to them.
- Forget what other people think. Even if they put you high on a pedestal for being a selfless carer. What they think doesn't matter as much as your future health.
- Challenge any sense of fatalism – the feeling that this is your

lot and you must stick with it. It is possible to make change happen, and that includes letting go.

Changing your role when someone goes to a care home

When you are telling neighbours or relations about the move to the care home, it often comes out as something that you have 'done to' your parent. This is reinforced by the negative views that people have about care homes.

I've seen all about care homes on the TV and I never want to go in one. Promise me you will never do that to me. (Astrid, 85)

A good care home can be a reward for a life well lived. It is a solution for older people who are lonely and afraid in their own homes. It is better than rushed visits four times a day from a variety of care staff who are lovely people and caring but are under pressure to get on to the next client.

I counted and in the last year of his life my husband had more than 120 different carers coming into the house to look after his personal hygiene. (Widow)

Care homes are well regulated and staffed by people with training and education who do this job because of the satisfaction they get from it. You will have chosen a care home that has all these qualities. There is good food and a nice private room and things to do each day. No one is perfect, but you can talk to them if things go wrong, and they will try to make it right. There is more about finding a care home and considering the alternatives in the companion volume to this book, *Care Homes: The One-Stop Guide: When, Why and How to Choose a Care Home*.

Never the less, there will be people who regard the move as you 'putting them away.' But in truth, you didn't cause this to happen. You helped the person to make the right choice and supported them to make sure that it went well. If they couldn't make the decision for themselves, you acted bravely and responsibly and made the decision on their behalf. Becoming frail and needing care beyond what anyone can provide at home is part of normal life for many more people as we live longer and longer. Some people are fortunate and never need it. For those who do need it, they are very lucky if they have someone like you who will make sure the transition goes as well as possible. When someone you care for goes to a care home you are taking on a new responsibility, not giving up on responsibility. Don't expect everyone to understand, though.

While you have been thinking about the care home, you will probably have had moments of sadness. It might be the right move, but it involves a lot of work and worry including sorting out finance, visiting homes, weighing up options. You have had to do all these things, perhaps on top of carrying out direct caring responsibilities. That is bound to make you weary. On the other hand you might now be thinking, 'Hurrah! Now I can go on holiday and not have to worry about them,' and feeling glad to be getting some of your life back.

It is likely that you will either feel somewhere in between, or even swing back and forth between the two poles. That is normal. Remember that in finding a safe and happy place for someone frail and dependent to live, you've done them a great service of care. You have done the best that you can.

You might have been soldiering on for a long time, not paying attention to your feelings. Ignoring stress affects your sleep and makes you more prone to illness. Even after the move into the care home, you may find you don't have the energy to start to take back some of the good things that you have been missing.

I've noticed recently when it gets towards the end of the day, I've been thinking that I deserve a large gin for what I'm going through. Then it began to be two or three. I'm supposed to be losing weight and watching my blood pressure, but after a couple of drinks I start ordering pizza deliveries. (Daughter)

Having to take care of yourself may have started to be yet another burden on top of caring for someone else, so you even feel guilty about not doing what you are 'supposed' to do for your own health like sleeping, eating, and exercising properly. At a time when you are making a major effort, you possibly believe that the care home move was a sort of failure. You are very short of time, and if the person you care for is moving to a care home this will rectify some of that. But not all of it and not immediately. Don't expect a miraculous improvement in your stress levels and your own well-being. Regard this as a success and be glad!

*I had noticed a difference between what seemed to be two sorts of families. In one place the children will say, 'We **succeeded in getting** our mum into a care home.' In another place they say, 'We **had to put** our mum in a care home.' It was clear that there was a different attitude because of the way they all thought about their local care homes. You can guess which area had the nice homes. (Social worker)*

Before the care home move, you may have been spending increasing amounts of time on hospital visiting or higher levels of caring duties and the transition feels sudden and unexpected. You find yourself with a hole in your daily routine. You may be able to think about a new structure for your day. There is a risk that you will fall into another punishing round of activity because you're not sure what to do when there is nothing you 'need' to do. Another danger is that you will spend all your time worrying about how the person is getting on, instead of letting go and allowing others to provide the basic care. It's the danger of 'over-caring'.

If someone has been a family carer for a long time, passing the person they care for on to someone else ought to feel like a relief, but many people find themselves worrying about how they'll settle, and whether they have done the right thing. For a time, sometimes a long time, they feel sad and lost about it. They might feel lonely. Families may be concerned about how often they 'ought' to visit, and what they ought to do when there. How should you be with the staff? Can you trust them? Are they kind? If you tell them what's needed, or ask them to do something different will they resent it? In some cases, these complex and overwhelming feelings are dismissed as 'guilt' about 'putting someone away'. That is an over-simplification of a very difficult transition for the family carers. It's unhelpful.

If you were undertaking most of the personal care yourself before, and your routine revolved around your caring duties, you will now have a time where you can start to look at other ways of giving structure and meaning to your days. It might involve visiting and taking the person out, but it might also involve going back to the work, leisure, friends, and entertainments you used to have before you were a carer. Some people feel guilty when they find they have more time for themselves.

I've forgotten what we used to do before we had to care for dad!
(Daughter of James, 76)

You can talk to family and friends about these feelings but sometimes that is too close, so you might prefer an online forum or another organisation that provides space to talk about how you are feeling. If you are overwhelmed with sadness you can talk to

Samaritans, or your GP may be able to put you in touch with a counsellor. You need to trust the people you are talking to so that you can be honest. Please remember that this is a great big transition for many people. Even if you have been managing this from the other end of the country as a long-distance carer, you may find yourself wondering what your role is now. It is confusing to feel glad and sad at the same time.

You may also be worried about whether the care is good enough for the one you love. That discomfort, being normal, is different from real concerns about possible abuse of the resident. Abuse is not common but does happen and you must be alert.

I am worried about how my father is being treated (Mark, son of James, 76)

Your relationship may seem to change when someone goes in a home but fundamentally this is the same person – your relative or friend. Feeling that you ought to be doing more and worrying whether the resident will be understood is one thing. A real concern about whether they are being harmed or neglected is something completely different.

He was sometimes sitting in dirty clothes, and the smell in the room wasn't good. He usually likes people, and he was telling me that he didn't like the care staff. I started to wonder if he was a bit scared, but he was certainly withdrawn. I could see that at times his food or drink had been left out of reach. In the end it was an unexplained bruise that made me act. I don't know why I didn't respond before. (Mark, son of James, 76)

There is no right or wrong way to feel about someone moving into care, but if you suspect they are being abused there are some correct actions you must take. Being afraid of staff, and signs of neglect are red flags. There are names of organisations you can talk to at the end of the book along with details of Hourglass helpline.

If you are feeling more energy, you will want to visit, but what expectations do people have of the frequency of your visits? And what do you do when you are there?

My wife was unable to talk, but she liked to see me. I would take her wheelchair out into the garden, and I'm not very good at doing nothing. Then I would talk to her, but I brought my gardening tools with me, and I would sort out the borders while keeping her company and she seemed to like watching me working. After she died, they still let me come and do the garden and I was glad of something to do. (Allan)

Some families still do a lot of care after the person has moved to the care home. They take advantage of the changed role.

We regard the care home as providing maintenance. It is our visits that provide the care. They feed and wash her. We are her source of life and love. (Sarah, sister of a care home resident)

Choosing a move to a care home is not 'putting someone away'. It is handing over some of the routine tasks, so that you can concentrate on what only you can do. The care home is required to provide social and recreational opportunities for residents. If being constantly present there is a reassurance for you, go ahead as much and as often as you like. But if it is exhausting, remember why the care home exists. It provides a constant presence in the life of the resident, so that you don't have to.

And if you have a sense that at last now you have help, don't forget that you still could use some more. Reserve time for yourself and prioritise. There's a risk that you start to throw yourself into a new regime that you could not maintain. Don't hesitate to ask for help with visiting from friends, family, neighbours, your faith community such as your church, or your social club like a veterans' association. They might wrongly imagine that the job is done already. It's not. Take help if it is offered, and even hire help, for example, someone who will provide companionship in the home when you are not able to visit. Your relationship is changing and that takes energy. Most of all, relax and catch up on sleep. Anyone who has managed a transition like this really deserves a good night's sleep.

Carers may have lost contact with friends and family and feel isolated because they have spent so much time on their caring tasks. It might be hard to think of getting in touch with people you used to know well and making new friends might be just as hard. What would you talk about?

Don't feel you have to rush. You need to do things as and when you feel like it. The people that you do have contact with might do or say awkward things. Their problem is that they don't know what to say, and they can't think where to start. It works best if you can tell them what they can do to support you. Remember that your friends and family can do a lot of this communication for you. Talking about what has happened can help. Many care homes have a residents' and relatives' group where you will meet other people who have gone through the same thing as yourself.

There is more about choosing a care home in *Care Homes* in this One-Stop Guide series of books.

When the person dies

The time frame of death for old, frail adults is uncertain. It is hard for anyone to know when this is approaching. Some older people die suddenly in the same way that younger people might. In old age it is more common to die after chronic ill-health.

When someone is diagnosed with cancer, families often immediately think about death. With dementia, which is a very common illness in older people, families often do not think about the fact that the person will die of dementia if they don't die of something else in the meantime. It is very rare for 'old age' to be recorded on the death certificate as a reason for death.

In the weeks before end of life you may notice a loss of appetite, general weakness and increasing fatigue. In the days before end of life the person will likely sleep more than they are awake. They move and talk less and may not respond to conversation. This is the time when we often say that an old person 'died in their sleep'. There may be many overlapping medical conditions, but it might require invasive testing to establish which one exactly was the final cause. You probably don't want that. It is just as if the biological clock has run down.

Many people say they would prefer to die at home in their own bed. If that can be managed, it is a comforting thing. But it is not always practical because in the final stages the person may need care at a level and intensity that families and the community nursing and medical team are not able to offer at home. If the death happens at home, call the GP as soon as possible. They will normally visit the house and, if the death was expected, should be able to issue a certificate there and then. You can then call a funeral director, who can take the person's body to the funeral home. If the doctor cannot give a certificate, the body will have to be taken to a hospital mortuary.

Everyone who loves other people will eventually be bereaved. The older you are, the more experience of death of a loved one you will have seen. There is no evidence that it becomes easier over time. Older people have been exposed to multiple deaths of family members and friends and they experience the same sorrow every time. No matter who they are, losing an older relative or friend is huge. Dealing with loss is never easy. My heart goes out to you if this is what has happened. All I can do is to offer practical advice that may help you at this time.

There are different ways of accessing **bereavement support**, such as:

- A local bereavement counsellor contacted via your GP.
- A charity for bereaved people in England, Wales and Northern Ireland called Cruse Bereavement Care, and Cruse Bereavement Care Scotland.
- Sue Ryder has online bereavement support which can connect you to one-to-one professional help, sharing with others in similar situations or finding information.
- Support from Carers UK.

All the contact details are in Useful Contacts and Resources.

There are very many practical issues after a death. A funeral director can arrange for the person to be collected and brought to their premises as soon as possible and can guide you all the way to making funeral arrangements.

Death certificate

The 'medical certificate of cause of death' or **death certificate** is a legal document that explains how someone died. If the cause of death is clear, this is usually issued by the doctor straight away.

My mother died in a care home and because she had not been seen by a doctor for quite a long time, they had to tell the Procurator Fiscal. He had to decide whether the cause of death was clear or whether a post-mortem was needed or whether to hold an inquest. This is bizarre. My mother had dementia, was 89 and had been unwell for years. In what world was this a suspicious death? (Daughter)

If the cause of death is not clear, or the person died unexpectedly or hadn't been seen by a doctor in the preceding two weeks, this information will be passed to the Coroner in England with a view to an inquest, or the Procurator Fiscal in Scotland where a Fatal Accident Inquiry could take place. This would mainly be if the cause of death is unknown, or if there is a suspicion that the person may have died a violent or unnatural death. Sometimes additional questions are asked if the person you are caring for died in hospital and you had reason to complain about their care before they died. In some cases a post-mortem examination is suggested.

Register the death

When someone dies you must **register the death** within five days in England, Wales and Northern Ireland or eight days in Scotland. This includes weekends and bank holidays. You can find the nearest register office by asking the funeral director, the doctor or the local council. Or you may find it online. After registration you will be given a certificate for a burial that is required by the funeral director, or an application for cremation which you as relative or executor need to complete and give to the crematorium. These things must be done before the funeral can take place.

Notify people and organisations

The list of people you must notify when someone dies includes relatives and friends, of course. You should tell the GP, and you might have to cancel any hospital appointments that are due.

Tell Us Once is a service in most of England and Wales that allows you to report a death to most government organisations in one go. (It is not available in Northern Ireland.) The registrar will help explain

this when you register the death. They will either complete it with
you or give you a unique reference number so you can use the service
yourself online or by phone. (Tell Us Once website)

You will need a long list of details. Already having this information in one place would be really useful.

- Date of birth
- Date they died
- National Insurance number
- Driving licence number
- Vehicle registration number
- Passport number
- State Pension details
- Benefit details
- Council services, including their Blue Badge
- Details of surviving spouse or civil partner (if you have their permission)
- Details of next of kin (if you have their permission)
- Details of the executor or administrator
- Details of public-sector or Armed Forces pension schemes

The **DWP (Department of Work and Pensions) Bereavement Service** allows you to report the death to the DWP in a single phone call which will cover all the benefits the person who died was getting. At the same time the Bereavement Service can do a benefit check to find out if the next of kin can claim any benefits and take a claim for bereavement benefits for a funeral payment over the phone. The contact details are at the end of this book.

In respect of the deceased person's financial affairs, you need to tell the bank and building society, insurance companies (including life, car and travel insurance) and the credit card provider. If they have a solicitor and accountant, tell them also.

*The **Death Notification Service** is a free online service which allows you to notify a number of member organisations about someone's death at the same time. (Death Notification Service website)*

It saves you having to contact lots of different organisations. You give the name and address, date of birth and date of death. You can give the date of the funeral and the death certificate number, but you don't need to, so why would you? You must identify yourself by name, address, contact number, date of birth and email address. You create an account and during the following ninety days you can add organisations to contact. There is a drop-down list from which you can choose. If you notify as many organisations as possible it is more efficient. You can print off a summary page that gives you a unique reference number which you should keep safely. It can reduce the overwhelming administrative burden when someone dies.

My top tip? Get multiple copies of the death certificate. You are going to need them. (Alistair, nephew of Adrian)

There are some processes for which you need proof of the death. If you are waiting for an inquest to finish you can get an **interim death certificate**. This is something you can use to apply for **probate**. What is probate? It's a legal right to deal with the person's estate after their death. You apply for a document which gives you access to their assets. It's not always needed if they only had savings.

Funeral arrangements

The **funeral** can usually only take place after the death is registered. You can pay for a funeral director to arrange a funeral for you or do it yourself. It is worth checking if the person who has died planned for their funeral through a pre-paid funeral plan or life insurance.

You may frequently see adverts on the television that give the impression that people are made to pay too much for a funeral. If you're hiring a funeral director, it's important to choose one who is a member of one of the organisations that have codes of practice, and that includes giving you a price list if you ask for it.

Some local councils have their own funeral services, for example for non-religious believers. **Humanists UK** (formerly known as the British Humanist Association) and **Institute of Civil Funerals** can also help with non-religious funerals and the details of how to contact them are at the end of this book.

The **Money Advice Service** has information about funeral costs and how to reduce them. You can apply for a funeral expenses payment if you have difficulty paying for the funeral. It will cover the cost of a simple funeral, but you may have to pay extra. There is more about funeral payments on the www. gov.uk website.

Other money matters

Your own tax, benefit claims and pension might change depending on your relationship with the person who died. The **Bereavement Support Payment** has replaced what was once known as the Widow's Pension.

You might have to deal with the will, money and property of the person who has died if you're a close friend or relative. The same www.gov.uk website can get you started on that.

Afterword

When caring ends you may feel tired and lonely, or you may feel liberated. It isn't wrong to be grateful when you put down a burden. However, most people feel at a loss. You may become conscious after years of caring that you have missed out on lots of experiences. You may be surprised to realise how much effort you had been putting into your caring role without noticing it. For a long time, the last thing you have been thinking about is yourself. You may have been living with missed meals, broken nights and stress. Unless you are brimming with health and energy, now is the time to see your doctor, especially if you have been bereaved.

To get the most from your GP visit, decide whether it is urgent or ask for a particular GP. If you've made a good relationship with one while you were caring they might be the best one to see now. Ask for a health check-up and take a list of any medications that you are on. Discuss the important things first. Remind them that you have been a carer, tell them how you are feeling and ask if they know of any sources of help or support.

You may decide to continue taking part in your local carers' group. As a former carer you will be most welcome. You may have made good friends and allies and have a lot to give – to share with people who are just starting out on their journey of caring. Perhaps you would rather reconnect with old friends who you have not been able to spend enough time with for ages.

If you have been out of the workplace for a while, you may be lacking in confidence to start looking for new work. Many organisations set out to recruit carers and former carers returning to work. They recognise the skills that you have developed and the value of the experience that you now carry with you.

If you do not want or need to take a paid job you may enjoy

volunteering. You are accustomed to being busy, and being busy helping other people is a continuation of what you have been doing. But make sure you don't end up over-caring. Make sure you have plenty of time for exercise, meeting friends, leisure activities that you have always enjoyed and even just sitting still doing nothing. The luxury of putting your feet up and watching a movie on the TV. The luxury of an afternoon nap.

In my professional life I have spent many hours listening to carers and discovering the sorts of problems that they face every day. The kindness and care that they give to older people is awesome. In a world where we are often concerned about ageism and discrimination against older people, the work done by family carers and friends is a lesson to us all.

Every holy book has something to say about caring for people in old age. For millennia we have known that older people feared ageing. Psalm 71:9 says 'And now in my old age, don't set me aside. Don't forsake me now when my strength is failing.' Muslims by faith are expected to care for older people. The Qur'an says, 'be kind to your parents. If either or both of them reach old age with you, do not even say "uf" to them or scold them, but speak to them in terms of honour and kindness. Lower to them the wing of humility, and say, "My Lord! Have mercy on them".'

An NHS Blessing song published in 2020 has beautiful words that work well for both family and friend carers. Play it to yourself from the website of the composer and singer Lucy Bunce (www.lucybunce.com). People of all faiths or no faith can take a moment to feel the love and support of these words:

Bless the hands that bless,
Now care for the ones who care.

Chapter 7

The Big List – An A to Z of Practical Hints

There is a lot in this book about the problems carers share with me when we talk to each other, problems I have experienced myself, both as a carer and when being cared for, and those things that show up most often in research about carers and what they live through. Other chapters demonstrate to you (as if you don't already know) what sort of things go wrong and the kind of problems carers have. This chapter is only about practical solutions. The entire focus is on answers and tips, although you will see more and different tips in other chapters. There are suggested solutions throughout the book so there may be some repetition, but this is the Big List. If you think any problems have been missed you can email me and tell me, and I'll make sure they are covered in the next edition and online on my website at www.juneandrews.net.

The ideas are in alphabetical order, and three handy hints for each of the issues or problems are listed after each one.

Assistive technology

'Assistive technology' or 'tech' is the expression for any device that helps make up for gaps in the older person's capability to be independent. It's a term often used to mean digital or electronic equipment. To be honest, a rubber glove that you use because it helps you to take the lid off jam jars is a kind of assistive technology. It doesn't have to be complicated or expensive. Or electronic. It can be for the benefit of the carer, to make their job easier. Otherwise it is for the person cared for, to make them more independent. A telephone would be regarded as 'tech' because it helps with communication. So there is low tech and high tech.

The benefit derived from electronic devices depends on the problem. For example, in dementia you might need prompts to help complete a task, or the family might need to have some idea of where the person is if they are likely to become lost. (See about **geofencing** below under 'Wandering'.) If the person has had a stroke, communication and mobility might be areas where an assistive technology solution could help.

Even if the person is healthy and largely independent they might appreciate some extra tech to make life easier, for example in reducing their anxiety about security by providing a video camera to check who is at the door, or a digital lock to control who has access to their house. Other tech might reduce loneliness in older people by helping them to keep in touch.

An **Alexa** or similar virtual assistant can control smart devices in the home, acting as a home automation system. To find out what is available and what might be helpful, look on the website of **AskSARA** at asksara.livingmadeeasy.org.uk. You will find information that is divided geographically, because what is available depends on where you live. The site takes you through a questionnaire about what you need and then suggests the most likely kit. Importantly, it provides some information about whether you can get it locally through your own local authority. If you need to buy or rent it, the site gives an idea of how much it costs and where you can get it.

The increase in the range of devices has not been as fast as one might have hoped. Rather than listening to what older people and their carers might need, there is a trend for inventors to invent things and then work out if there is a market for them among older, frail people and carers. That's good, but not good enough. People need to listen to carers. It's not self-sacrifice. A real understanding of the size of the market might make inventors and producers think harder about how they can make money by making life easier for others. Everyone would win.

A **home automation system** can control lighting, heating, access and alarm systems. They have been around for a long time, but more recently have the added benefit that the carer can control them remotely using a smartphone. They allow family members to share information about personal security or environmental information, such as how warm the home is.

From time to time I see that Dad has been economising on the energy again, and I can turn on his heating from my phone and make sure that his house doesn't get chilly. At first he thought it was like 'big brother is watching', but now he hardly notices. (Ellen, daughter of Alf)

There are sometimes concerns about the dignity and privacy of the older person when someone else can control their environment. You need to get the consent of the person you are caring for. The system can be designed to let a carer know online where the person is in their house. It's not like closed-circuit TV, where you would be seen on cameras. Instead, a movement sensor records activity and how long you spend in each room and alerts the carer if the pattern is wrong.

I can look at my computer or smartphone and see what Mum's been doing. I can see that she has spent a lot of the day in the living room and pottering between the toilet and kitchen. If she was to go into the toilet and not come out for half an hour, I'd get an alert. I could call her, or phone her neighbour to go round and see if she has fallen in there and is stuck. Even when I'm working overseas I can check that she's OK and doing her normal thing. (Kisha, daughter of Amina, 87)

The most common sort of assistive technology that is provided by local authorities is **telecare**. A typical example would be an emergency call system that is operated by a pendant worn round the neck. Other technology that they may provide is focused on reducing risk, so this includes **fall detectors, gas and smoke alarms** and devices for shutting off water and gas. The local fire department will come and check alarms for older people free of charge. For security a common device is the key safe, which allows appropriate visitors or care workers to access the person's home without having keys circulating in the community. As a carer, if you do not live with the person or are out at work you can arrange to have the door controlled using a remote camera and a lock that is operated from your smartphone, to allow you to monitor visitors and let them in.

Other locks use fingerprint identification. These devices can monitor who has been in and out of the house and for how long. It is not unknown for care workers to mislead clients about how long they spend caring. In addition, if the care worker, through no fault of their own, is prevented from calling in it can set up an early warning alert to the carer. It sometimes happens that the care system breaks down and no one knows in good time that a person has missed a visit from the care worker who should help them to bed or make their lunch. With such a lock, you'd know and could be alerted.

Assistive technology is also useful for reminiscence and for puzzles and games. In the past, an older person might not naturally have reached for their iPad or home computer for this sort of entertainment, but increasingly they now do. Especially since the pandemic, older people have increased their use of Facetime and other apps to keep in touch with family and each other. People rarely use all the complex features that are on an ordinary house phone, but you will be able to block callers and minimise the risk to the older person if you can find the instruction manual. (Top tip: you will find it online if your relative has mislaid it.)

Three hints

1. Tech changes all the time, so look at websites for the latest
2. Sometimes the local authority will pay, so ask them what they've got
3. The sooner you have tech in your own life, the easier it will be when you are old

Bathing in the bathroom

Keeping the person clean is not just about hygiene but also about upholding dignity and maintaining the health of their skin. The challenges of this kind of intimate care are explored elsewhere in the book. But if you're going to do it, here are some ideas.

How often do you have to do it? Remember, this is mainly about an older person who cannot or will not attend to their own hygiene.

You normally don't need to give someone a bath or a shower more than twice a week, but aim for that at least. Every day they should be helped to wash their face, and down below, front and back. And of course, it's important to help them to wash their hands every time they use the toilet and before eating. (District nurse)

If the person can wash themselves, your main challenge is to assess the bathroom for safety. Make sure it is difficult for the person to lock themselves in – you may have to get into the bathroom if there is a fall or other accident.

Mum fell behind the bathroom door. It was unlocked but we still couldn't get in. I called an ambulance and Charles had to go up a ladder and break through the bathroom window. Without such a good neighbour, we would have had to call the fire brigade. (Mark)

Asking yourself a 'What if?' set of questions is a risk assessment. Life has some risks, and you have to accept that fact if the person is fiercely independent.

Use the central control thermostat to fix the hot water temperature at the central boiler and prevent scalding accidents. There is further guidance about safety in the bathroom under 'Home adaptations' including advice on flooring, steps, stools and rails.

Sometimes the person is very pleased to be given a hand, but it is a real problem if they resist taking a bath or shower. It just seems like too much work for them and too much fuss. You can try to approach it in a way that makes it seem more fun, but remember that many older people may have been brought up on far fewer baths than we have now. It is not worth making it a battleground.

Begin by assembling everything that you need, including towels and the clothing that they will be putting on after the bath.

My mother was very clever. The care home staff could never get Granny to have a wash. When Granny needed a bath, my mother never asked her because she would always say no. She would just lead her towards the bathroom making conversation all the way. There was a great performance of showing Granny the new clean clothes that she was going to put on and asking her what she thought about them. In the process, my mother would be starting to undress Granny before manoeuvring her into the bath. Granny really enjoyed the experience, even though she refused every time she was asked. (J, daughter of D, daughter-in-law of M)

Having a bath can be more luxurious than a shower, but it is sometimes hard to get someone in and out of the bath if they have arthritis or other mobility problems. You can buy a **side entry bath**, but more commonly people make do with a shower because it is less expensive and disruptive. If you're helping the person to shower it is easier and safer if they will sit down on a specially designed **shower stool**. You can get a folding one fitted to the wall of the shower. Wearing shower shoes with grips to prevent slipping makes it even safer. Particularly if the person has dementia or is nervous, they may be alarmed by feeling shower water coming down on their head and a detachable showerhead that you can use to spray water gently around their body is much less stressful. If the person gets stressed they won't co-operate, and it is more likely that there will be a fall or other problem. The website bathingwithoutabattle.unc.edu offers tips on bathing equipment and technique. See the listing in Useful Contacts and Resources in the 'Information about caring' section.

Explanation is important, and lots of encouragement. You can buy a **towelling modesty garment** that is open at the back which the person continues to wear even when they're under the water, so their nakedness is never exposed throughout the process. It can be left behind in the shower cubicle or bath when they step into a dry towelling robe or large bath towel to get dry. A seat or recliner in the bath can help the person to feel secure. Bath time can be a relaxing and pleasant experience, enhanced by having some nice music playing. Or it can be a battleground.

When a confused person is resisting being washed, they may be usefully distracted if you give them something to hold. If they are clutching a washcloth or a sponge they are less likely to use their hands to try and push away the other cloth that you are using to wash them down.

If bathing in the bathroom is too difficult, it is possible to give someone a perfectly good wash in bed or in their chair. By putting a towel under each limb in turn you can give the person a rubdown with a soapy flannel and use another one to rinse. Some of the products which you will see for sale for people who are going to music festivals or camping can be put to good use in the circumstances. They are available online or from large chemists and they include large body wet wipes and 'no rinse' body wash foam. You squirt the foam on and rub it off with a towel. Just like that. Clean and smelling good.

One area of personal hygiene never to miss is the hands and mouth. Make sure hands are washed before food and after the toilet, and keep nails trimmed and clean. Clean teeth twice a day. There is more advice under the heading 'Mouth care'.

Get advice about toenails as they may be best left to a podiatrist. If it is possible to get genitals and bottom cleaned each day, that's going to make life nicer for everyone, even if a bath or shower is not possible. If you reach the stage where this is not going to happen, that's when you might have to consider getting help.

For hair, you can buy a product which looks like a shower cap. These **no-rinse shampoo caps** are full of 'no-rinse' shampoo and you put the hat on the person's head and massage the hair. When you take it off you can towel-dry the hair – a really simple way to get clean, fresh-smelling hair. Washing the hair over the sink is easier than in the bath or shower, but the cap is even simpler and it can be therapeutic massaging someone's head for five to ten minutes. Or you can take the person to a hairdresser, and if they're familiar with the salon they will find it entertaining or even comforting. Many hairdressers will work in a person's home and that's even easier. Talk to your local hairdresser. Or, in the case of gents, their barber.

Three hints

1. Safety first
2. Use products to keep life simple
3. Don't let bathing cause a battle; dirt isn't all bad

Benefits

The main discussion of benefits is in Chapter Three. You need up-to-date advice from a current **benefits calculator** on a website. You should treat your results as a helpful estimate to start to figure out what you could be claiming. A calculator cannot guarantee your eligibility for any benefit or tax credits, so contact the relevant department to confirm your entitlement. To fill in the benefit calculator online form you need to have some information to hand, including details of income and savings, investments and other capital, Council Tax bill, rent or mortgage repayments and details of any benefits you already claim.

Calculators can be found at:

- *Turn2us* – for information on income-related benefits, tax credits, Council Tax Reduction, Carer's Allowance, Universal Credit and how your benefits will be affected if you start work or change your working hours. benefits-calculator-2.turn2us. org.uk

- *Policy in Practice* – for information on income-related benefits, tax credits, contribution-based benefits, Council Tax Reduction, Carer's Allowance, Universal Credit, how these are calculated and how your benefits will be affected if you start work or change your working hours. www.betteroffcalculator.co.uk

● *Entitledto* – for information on income-related benefits, tax credits, contribution-based benefits, Council Tax Reduction, Carer's Allowance, Universal Credit and how your benefits will be affected if you start work. www.entitledto.co.uk

● *Age UK* – provides either an estimate or an indication of possible eligibility for a range of benefits. benefitscheck.ageuk.org.uk/ Home/Start

● *Carers Trust* – should link with Working Tax Credit, Child Tax Credit, Pension Credit, Housing Benefit, Council Tax Support, Child Benefit, Income Support, Jobseeker's Allowance, Employment and Support Allowance or Universal Credit. carers.org/money-and-benefits/benefits-calculator

Other websites can give you up-to-date information on issues such as Carer's Allowance, DLA (Disability Living Allowance), PIP (Personal Independence Payments), Bedroom Tax, benefit caps etc. Most usefully, Carers UK has advice on challenging a benefit decision.

I am so sorry I cannot make it any simpler. If you need a pal to talk you through this, remember that Age UK, Citizens Advice and other organisations offer face-to-face support.

There are local carer organisations throughout the UK that can help.

Free money matters surgeries for carers. Carers have so many things to think about – why not book an appointment at VOCAL's free carer advice surgeries and let a specialist adviser help you? To book an appointment, please get in touch. We provide support for carers in Edinburgh and Midlothian. Visit one of our Carer Centres for advice and support in person. Our Carer Support Workers continue to provide support face-to-face over video calls or over the phone or contact you by email. (VOCAL – an active member of the Coalition of Carers in Scotland)

Three hints

1. The website is your friend
2. Chapter Three of this book should help
3. Organisations like Age UK, Carers UK and Citizens Advice are great

Blue Badge

Having a Blue Badge card is a tremendous benefit when you are going out and about with the person you are caring for. That's the badge that gives you the right to park closer to your destination, often in a designated spot for Blue Badge users. Unfortunately, so many people have misused this service that it takes a while to get approval (up to twelve weeks) and it is sometimes tedious trying to get a badge. If you want to apply for one, the details are here on the government website at www.gov.uk/apply-blue-badge. The pass usually lasts for three years, and you must apply for a new one before the current badge expires. It is linked to the person who is being cared for rather than a vehicle, so it can be used in any car by anyone who is transporting that person while they are travelling as a passenger. Or they can use it themselves if they are still driving.

The badge usually lets you park free on streets with parking meters or pay-and-display machines, but you have to check for local variations. The badge holder can also park on single or double yellow lines for up to three hours in many places. You can ask the local council to create a **special disabled space** outside your home. Your GP will be able to provide information that helps the application, especially if you are registered as a carer.

Three hints

1. Get registered as a carer with your GP
2. Apply for the badge
3. Reapply in good time

Bowels and urine

When caring for someone else, you end up being involved in topics you've never discussed in your whole life. Sometimes people don't even have the same words for what is being discussed. Talking about urination and defecation, passing water and opening the bowels, peeing and pooing, is hard enough. Dealing with it when it goes wrong is another level of complexity altogether. Aside from the practicalities, you have to deal with the potential shame and embarrassment of the person you are caring for, and your own mixed feelings. If you can remain calm and understanding it helps, but this can be a challenge if the older person resists your attempts to assist. This is one of the issues that can tip the decision to get professional help and may precipitate the person having to move into a care setting.

I felt much better when I admitted how uncomfortable I was with this. Even though I was given products that made some things easier, I realised I just couldn't change my relationship with my mother and become so intimate at this late stage in our lives. I realised then that we needed outside help. (Kisha, daughter of Amina)

Some people do manage, but it is understandable when they can't. Incontinence is when a person is unable to go to the toilet in the right place at the right time. It is not inevitable in old age, but many conditions that are more common in older people make incontinence more likely. So, for example if a person has arthritis or mobility problems, they may have difficulty getting to the toilet on time. If repeated episodes of incontinence occur, you should ask for an assessment from the GP. They might make a referral to a hospital urology clinic, and they may ask for the continence nurse adviser to see the person. This is a registered nurse with extensive training who can assess the condition and develop a management plan to suit the needs of the person you are caring for. They might visit them at home or see them in the clinic. Don't just assume incontinence is part of normal ageing.

From a practical point of view, how you manage it depends on what is causing the continence problem. Sometimes there is medicine that can help. At other times it can really make a difference if you just remind the person to go to the toilet frequently. There may be a temporary problem, such as a urinary tract infection, which makes it hard for the person to hold their water. In that case the situation might resolve itself after the infection has been treated. You will get advice from the clinical staff, but it is always the case that drinking more water and staying hydrated is good for the person. Logically, it might seem that you avoid having leaks by not drinking very much, but the opposite is the case.

Anyone who becomes dehydrated is more likely to get a bladder infection, and that leads to irritation that can cause a person to wet themselves. Everyone should keep their pee straw-coloured by taking lots of fluid. If it gets any darker you are not drinking enough or you have an infection. Often you can tell there is an infection because there is a distinctive smell, and the urine is dark and cloudy no matter how much you drink. Follow your nose. If a person's underwear or the toilet are smelly, that's a clue. This is true for yourself as well as the person you care for.

Nursing staff can give advice about **plastic bed covers, waterproof garments, adapted swimwear, continence pads** and other items that protect linen and furnishings. Skin care is very important. The skin surface can break down with prolonged contact just like the painful nappy rash that children can have. The skin must be kept clean and dry. To find out more about the products that can help with this, look at the independent website www.continenceproductadvisor.org

The design of the toilet makes a difference. The seat may have to be raised to reach the correct height, and grab rails needed to steady the person and give them confidence to sit. If a person has the right shoes on and the floor coverings are appropriate, they can make their way to the toilet faster. If they have too many zips and fastenings, layers of tights and knickers and other clothing to get off they may not be able to get to the toilet in time. Sometimes just thinking about going to the toilet can make the need more urgent. If the toilet is too far away or on the wrong floor of the dwelling you may need to acquire a **commode**, which is a portable toilet.

See more in 'Equipment for household tasks' below.

If all else fails, a man may be provided with a **penile sheath**. This rolls on to his penis like a condom but has a collecting tube and a bag to collect urine, so it can be regularly emptied down the toilet. Keeping it clean is important. It might only be worn at certain times, for example in bed at night, if getting to the loo in time is difficult. Another device which can be used by men or women is a **urinary catheter**, which is inserted inside the bladder by the nurse and stays there with the tube coming out of the urethra. A bag is attached which collects the urine for disposal later. Hygiene is vital with these devices because they make the person vulnerable to urinary tract infections. The nurse who inserts it should show you how to keep it clean.

Dealing with faecal (poo) incontinence is another issue. Clinical staff can tell a lot about someone's health from their poo. The shape, colour, consistency and form give evidence about what you have eaten and whether your gut is coping with it. Even floating stools (poo) tell you something. If the person does less than three bowel movements in a week, that is viewed as constipation. That's all very interesting for me as a nurse, but from a carer's point of view the most urgent thing is what you do if it ends up in the wrong place at the wrong time.

The first thing is to tidy up the problem and the second is to see if it can be prevented from happening again. Again, it is not an inevitable part of ageing. Culturally this is a very hard task, even if you have often already cheerfully done it for small children, or even a puppy.

It's a good idea to have some disposable gloves which you throw away after cleaning up poo from the person, their linen, or from hard surfaces such as the bathroom floor or toilet seat. Reusable rubber gloves are OK if you wash and disinfect them after each use. If you don't have gloves, wash your hands thoroughly with soap and water, but also wash your hands after you take off gloves. If the person has faeces on their skin use damp paper towels or kitchen roll or non-alcohol wet cleansing wipes to wipe off the poo and put those in a rubbish bag. Wash the person with warm water and a soft cloth. Only use soap if water doesn't do it, and make sure it is mild. If their skin is already red or has a rash, be sure not to use any wipes with alcohol as that will be very sore. Rinse well and dry carefully. Pat, don't rub. Then throw away the gloves, wipes etc. When wiping stool off linen or clothes, if you can pick off pieces of it with toilet paper you can flush that down the toilet. Otherwise wipe with paper towels which you put in the rubbish bag and wash the clothes in hot water, using household laundry detergent and adding laundry bleach to the cycle if you wish.

The same technique for hard surfaces cleans away solid

material, and then you can use whatever bleaching agent or anti-bacterial spray is normal for that surface. For fabric surfaces like chairs or rugs, use the same technique to get the poo off then wash the area with laundry cleaner. Use a white cloth or paper towel and dab at the stain to remove it. A white cloth helps you see when you need to shift to a different bit of the cloth as it lifts the dirt. After it dries you can disinfect it with a suitable product spray, checking first that it will not discolour the rug or fabric. In care homes and other places where such accidents happen they buy chairs and floor coverings that look and feel like ordinary fabric, but which repel all fluids and dirt. You might consider this.

There is more information like this on the website of the **Bladder and Bowel Community** (www.bladderandbowel.org), which supports millions of people in the UK who are living with conditions that affect their bladder or bowel. For when you are out and about, through that site you can order a **'Just Can't Wait' toilet card**. This is credit card-sized and states that the holder has a medical condition which means they need to use a toilet quickly. This is extremely useful. Also they can tell you about the **National Key Scheme** that offers people who need it independent access to locked 'accessible' public toilets around the country.

Three hints

1. Always ask for a clinical assessment; treatment might cure it
2. Get help from the right people; they have solutions
3. For some people this is too much; that's not your fault

Choking

If you've ever done a first aid course you already know what to do if someone is choking. Older people have a higher choking risk than other people. They naturally produce less saliva, so chewing and swallowing food becomes more difficult. If their teeth are not very good or they have ill-fitting dentures this adds to the problem. If they have Parkinson's disease or have had a stroke or have dementia, that will affect their chewing and swallowing ability.

You will have heard of the **Heimlich Manoeuvre**. In the event of an incident stand behind the person with your arms around their waist. Bend them forward and put your fist above the bellybutton and pull sharply inwards and upwards. Repeat this a few times. If that doesn't clear the blockage you need to dial 999. You can purchase a device that uses suction to pull fluid or food out of the person's mouth, clearing their airway. This is advertised as a piece of kit that someone can use on themselves.

To avoid the need for this adventure, encourage the person to take time eating and avoid talking or drinking while chewing. Certain foods are known to trigger coughing or choking. They include dry meat and chicken, raw vegetables, nuts, seeds and dried fruits. Large medicine tablets can also be hard to swallow.

I am proud to say that I have twice helped someone who was choking using the Heimlich Manoeuvre. It worked both times. I shook like a leaf afterwards and wondered if they minded me manhandling them, but both were grateful that their life had probably been saved. I'd only ever seen it in a diagram. And they were strangers in a public restaurant both times. So you will definitely be able to do it if you need to.

If someone has difficulty swallowing, they should seek medical advice early because there may be treatment to help with the symptoms. Early investigation rules out other more serious conditions like oesophageal cancer. If tiny bits of food or fluid go down the wrong way, it can lead to chest infections such as pneumonia. Pneumonia is a medical emergency and you should call NHS111 immediately.

Ask the GP for a consultation with a **speech and language therapist (SALT)**. It's a misleading name because assessing swallowing is one brilliant area of their expertise. And a dietician to see what diet changes could help. Liquids might be easier to swallow if they are thickened, and soups if they are blended. Sitting up properly at the table to eat and keeping distractions to a minimum while eating can make a difference. Sometimes the person, having had a fright, avoids some vital foods and exists on things like ice cream and custard. If they become weaker as a result, they will be even less able to control their swallowing.

Three hints

1. Get help with early signs of swallowing problems
2. Use the SALT (speech and language therapist)
3. Doing a Heimlich Manoeuvre is easier than you think.

Cleaning

Many of the practical things that you can do to make it easier to clean the house of the person you are caring for are the same as the things you do to try and reduce the risk of them falling and to help them be independent. Getting rid of clutter can make a huge difference to how easy it is to clean up.

I know that real hoarding is where the amount of clutter interferes with everyday living, for example the person is unable to use the kitchen or bathroom and can't access rooms because of the junk. But my dad is verging towards that. Every time I go to clean up his kitchen I give up in disgust because I don't know where to put everything and there is just so much stuff everywhere. (Ellen, daughter of Alf, 79)

You can't go into someone else's house and start removing things and throwing them away or otherwise disposing of them without their permission. It may be that this house has just become too difficult for Alf to take care of and he doesn't have the energy to reorganise himself. If Ellen can persuade him that his life will be so much easier if he has a sort-out and she can do it with his co-operation, then so much the better.

If the person has dementia or cognitive impairment it helps them if you remove things that they are not using. An example is tidying up the kitchen so that the only things visible are those things that he uses every day, such as his kettle and a small range of cooking utensils. He will find it much easier to cook for himself. Putting what he needs behind glass-fronted cupboards so that he can see them is helpful. You can just take the cupboard doors off, and then things are visible on open shelves. This works best if all the unnecessary things are taken away with the person's permission. It's a good idea to hang on to the stuff for a short time in case they forget having given you that permission and start to worry where the things have gone.

Removing rugs and mats that are trip hazards makes it easier to clean floors.

Every time we went to see him, my sister or I would spend a small amount of time in the kitchen just wiping down some surfaces and doorhandles. I couldn't clean his grill and the inside of his fridge, which was gruesome, because even if I had time he would resist. I asked my brother to help and he took Dad out for the day fishing and left my sister and myself behind and we did a real deep clean together. We got rid of out-of-date food from his freezer and ancient items from his cupboard. There were fruit flies crawling round old pots of jam. Dad was bemused when we returned, but he soon settled and was happy to find how neat everything was and that his cupboards were full of fresh food that he found attractive and easy to prepare. And he had more new jam. (Ellen, daughter of Alf, 79)

If your mum was always house-proud, it may be very uncomfortable if your dad lets the housekeeping go. But as long as it is not exactly insanitary you may just have to relax and let him be. It's not a housekeeping competition and no one is judging you by the way his house looks. (I know that daughters feel shame. But relax about it. People who matter know what is going on. Other people don't matter.) If something needs doing for safety, prioritise that and ask for help. Even better, persuade him to get a cleaner for himself.

Three hints

1. Anyone who judges your caring by the state of the house knows nothing
2. Decluttering helps
3. Get a cleaner (Somehow. I know it is not easy.)

Clothing

Choosing the right clothing can make a difference to someone's independence. Casual clothes have become much more common recently as fewer people have been going to offices. Those clothes make it easier for people to dress and undress. At last, we have realised that clothing is much more about being comfortable than appearance. However, a previous generation may still value the 'shirt, tie and jacket' more formal dress. It is well known that some older people, particularly gentlemen, have favourite articles of clothing that they like to wear again and again. Poor eyesight might mean that he cannot see that his trousers are covered in stains. Women are more inclined to wear different clothes from day to day, allowing clothes to be laundered. When your dad wants to wear the same things all the time, a good solution is to get identical sets of the same clothes so that even if there is one in the wash, they are wearing one and there's another one in the wardrobe. They can wear the same outfit every day. Like Simon Cowell or Barak Obama. The very definition of cool.

Sometimes dressing someone is faster than allowing them to dress themselves, but it is better only to do this in emergencies. Care staff are encouraged to allow the person to dress themselves. You yourself have to do what you have to do. If the person has dementia, they may not choose the right clothes for the weather. You can lay out clothes for someone to dress themselves, or if you are with them hand them the items one by one. If you can put away some unseasonable clothes in a place that is less accessible, you reduce the likelihood of the wrong clothes being chosen. Fastenings like Velcro, large zippers and elasticated waistbands make it simpler for people to take their clothes on and off themselves. Slip-on shoes with Velcro fasteners make life easier.

As well as dressing for comfort, people must dress for safety. Ill-fitting slippers and shoes are a recipe for disaster, causing slips and trips. A dressing gown that is too long is likely to cause a fall when someone is moving about inside the house.

I had to confiscate my dad's shoes because they were so worn down at the heel it was twisting his ankles and affecting his gait. He kept saying there was still good wear in them and there was nothing wrong with the uppers. I put them in the bin but found next week he had fished them out and was wearing them again. And the wrong trousers. (Craig, son of Gerald, 98)

Older people do not feel the cold as younger people do and may not wear enough clothes in winter. Deaths from hypothermia in colder parts of the country in bitter winters are not uncommon. With climate change and some desperately hot days, we may also discover that older people are having difficulty in surviving in the heat and dressing appropriately for that. In 2020 an average of 9,700 deaths each year are believed to be caused by living in a cold house in the UK. Not having enough money for fuel, or even imagining that you don't have enough money for fuel, is the basic reason. If the person you care for is inclined to economise on the heating, making sure they have warm clothes goes some way towards protecting them.

Three hints

1. There are ways of supporting an older person to dress themselves
2. Putting away the 'wrong trousers' helps
3. Getting cold in winter is a serious issue

Cooking

The older person you care for may still be able to cook as they always did, and just require some modifications in the kitchen. You can see ideas in greater detail under 'Home adaptations'. This includes ideas for gas cut-off mechanisms for cookers and other safety features to prevent fire, flood and scalding. You may be helping them with shopping and using the advantages of online shopping to get their groceries delivered. Managing the finances of that with digital banking is easier if you get a shared account (see Chapter Three).

The real problems start with someone who cannot or will not cook. It may be an issue of skill or of motivation. If someone won't cook, they may be able to do quite well with cold food. The motivation to eat is what matters. If someone is motivated they will find a way to feed themselves. That can be affected by depression. Older people also lose appetite because of loss of sense of smell and taste, and there is more about this under 'Eating well'.

The house is so empty since your mother died and I really don't feel like eating very much. So I just make myself a sandwich now and again. (Dan, 76)

There are machines that can make cooking easier. If you are supporting an older person who still wants to learn and they've not used these gadgets, you can introduce them to the delights of the microwave, slow cooker, a George Foreman-type grill, a soup maker, a microwave grill and a blender. Demonstrations of what you can do with all these are on YouTube.

It is not unusual for an older person to have a small appetite. That means what they do eat absolutely must be packed with nutrients including sugars and fats. Many of us have been on slimming diets, and the advice for helping older people to eat well is the exact opposite of what we would do to lose weight. Make sure that easy-to-consume snacks are visible in the house to tempt them, and that includes high-calorie foods. Unintended weight loss is common in older people. They need to have protein, fat and carbohydrates as well as vitamins in their diet and presenting that combination in small portions is a skill in itself. Therefore, pre-prepared meals from supermarkets can be very useful. Because they have the ingredients listed, you can choose small ones which are packed with fat and protein.

Bad decisions sometimes happen because of a poor understanding of 'healthy eating'.

I have a healthy breakfast, though; of porridge I make for myself and tea. (Dan, 86)

Porridge is a healthy food. It fills you up and contains roughage, which is good for your gut and especially your bowels. But Dan's recipe is made of oats and water and his tea is black, because he doesn't get fresh milk in, so he's really on a slimming regime. Also, it is sixteen hours between his last meal at 6 p.m. and his breakfast when he gets up at 10 a.m. Over sixteen hours the person becomes ketotic, which means he is breaking down any fat stores he has in his body and, if it goes on long enough, also breaking down the protein in his muscles. So he's losing weight even if he eats well during the rest of the day. He is accidentally doing the new 16:8 fasting diet. That's good if he is fat, but Dan is not. The practical tip is to get him to have snacks by his bed to eat when he wakes during the night, and to have a chocolate biscuit or banana before he goes to bed, to break that fasting cycle. Dan's porridge would be better if he made it with milk and added extra cream, but research shows that the timing of meals is also important.

If the elderly person that you are caring for does not have extensive cooking skills, they can survive very well on food and drink that is simple to prepare. It depends what the person likes, but here are some more ideas for the fridge and stock cupboard:

- Cartons of smoothie
- Bottles of freshly squeezed juices
- Tins and cartons of soup (some can be consumed without heating)
- Ready meals from the high-end ranges, which are loaded with fat and calories
- Nice fruit, such as bananas, or small cartons of ready-chopped fresh fruit salad
- Cheese and bread to make toasted sandwiches with a toaster bag in the toaster
- Bags of green salad, ripe tomatoes, carrot sticks

- Pickles, potato salad, slices of cold meat, pork pies
- Slices of bacon and sausages for a quick fry-up
- Eggs to boil or scramble
- Mini trifles or tiny syrup puddings to microwave
- A tin of favourite chocolate biscuits
- Tins of sardines to have on toast
- Lots and lots of nice, tasty foods

Ready meals can be bought from the supermarket or an online delivery service, which you can arrange to be delivered on behalf of the person you care for. It is no longer unusual for supermarkets to deliver groceries to a person's house. If the older person is unable to operate a microwave oven, then you may be able to arrange for carers to come in and heat up a meal for them.

When I am batch-cooking for myself and the family at the weekend, I prepare some extra portions and drop them off at my mother's. She puts some in the fridge and she will heat them up for herself in the evenings if she is too tired to cook. Sometimes, when she is feeling more energetic, she just puts them into the freezer for later and makes something for herself. (Jolene)

As a carer you may scarcely have time to cook for yourself, but it may be that the person you are looking after can afford to have hot food delivered from a local café or restaurant, such as a tasty fish and chips on Friday or a delicious Chinese takeaway on Saturday night.

Interaction during meals improves the appetite. If they can go out to a supermarket or café for an affordable lunch, they are much more likely to eat well if they meet someone there. You may be able to arrange for a buddy to go for lunch with them at a regular interval. If the person you care for has been in the Armed

Forces, there are veteran organisations all over the country which will make a point of taking old soldiers out for a meal where, as comrades together, they can discuss their National Service or their time serving their country. Churches and community centres organise lunch clubs for retired people.

Three hints

1. Safety first
2. Not cooking is OK – eat like a picnic
3. Going out for food is good, and so is home delivery

Delirium

There are some medical emergencies that obviously need first aid. Choking or bleeding are examples. However, if the person you are caring for has an abrupt change involving emotional disturbance and fluctuating mental confusion, you must call a doctor. It could be a sign of delirium, which can happen when the person is coming down with an infection or is stressed and dehydrated. In older people the cause is most commonly a chest infection or a urine infection. Make sure you tell the medics how the person normally is and that this is an unexpected deterioration from their usual state. Problems arise when they assume that the older person you care for is always like this, or has a chronic condition like dementia, and don't investigate or try to reverse the underlying cause. Even if the person already has dementia, delirium can make them temporarily worse, and it's good to get that reversed, making your life and theirs easier.

If you are caring at home, it helps that the surroundings are familiar. The symptoms can be made worse by an unfamiliar environment. So if they are in hospital, you can try to recreate that by bringing in familiar objects and staying with the patient as much as you can. It is now possible to stay as long as you want if the person already has dementia, mainly as a result of the **John's Campaign**, which fought to allow open-access visiting. During the COVID-19 pandemic there was a clear demonstration of what happens to older people with delirium when separated from people they know. It was tragic. Making sure that they have their glasses and hearing aid can help to reduce confusion.

If it is possible to keep the person moving, that can help. Not least because it reduces constipation, which can make delirium worse. Remember that delirium can last for a long time. It could be months before the person gets really better, and many people die within a year. In literature delirium is often portrayed as a person who is raving, but in real life they sometimes lie quietly, drifting in and out of consciousness.

The staff said that my mum was 'no trouble' and sleeping most of the day. That was a warning sign for me. My mum is always trouble. If she was lying still, she must be really ill. I kept asking and they found she had a raging infection, even though there was no raised temperature. She was delirious. (Abby, daughter of Mary, 63)

Dehydration is common in settings like hospitals where it is warm and staff sometimes forget to provide fresh water or leave it within reach. Water is essential for the function of the brain and to prevent constipation. I despair at how hard it can be to encourage confused people to drink it. You can help.

Three hints

1. Being suddenly more confused is not normal for older people
2. Make sure the clinicians take it seriously
3. Keeping hydrated helps with most things

Dementia

You could write a book about how to care for a person with dementia. In fact, you don't have to because you can just read *Dementia* in the One-Stop Guide series. A significant percentage of older carers are looking after a spouse with dementia. It is vital to obtain as much information as possible about the condition so that you can get the help you need to make life easier for yourself and the person that you're looking after. You will still find yourself being a carer even if they're admitted to a care home or into hospital, because contact with family is crucial for care that is provided by professional caregivers. Dementia is sometimes also known as Alzheimer's disease, and the Useful Contacts and Resources chapter has contact details of organisations which are there to help people affected by the condition, including family and friends.

It is often presented as a 'memory problem'. Research has shown that for carers of people with dementia, there are at least six problems that require help which are even more problematic than not being able to remember things. These are aggression, anxiety, sleeplessness, wandering, repeatedly calling out and depression. There is detailed advice on dealing with all these dementia-related problems in *Dementia: The One-Stop Guide*. It also explores how to get a diagnosis and what to do in a wide range of situations that occur, such as when the person becomes lost or is in hospital. There are legal problems that can arise with money. What should you do when a person with dementia has no insight and will not agree to get a diagnosis? It can't be done in a couple of paragraphs here, but there is more on the website at www.juneandrews.net and in the book.

Three hints

1. Information is power
2. Read *Dementia: The One-Stop Guide*
3. Dementia carers can get help from organisations listed in Useful Contacts and Resources

Depression

In Chapter Five, which is about your own health, there is good information about why carers like yourself might become depressed and what you can do about it. It is not only the carer who may suffer from depression but also the person they are caring for. Even people whose main diagnosis is dementia may benefit from depression treatment, including medication and talking therapy. You can ask your GP whether medication would improve the person's mental state. You cannot force anyone to get help if they don't want it, but if you are registered as a carer and have welfare power of attorney that allows the GP to discuss the person with you. Under other circumstances they can't because of patient confidentiality.

Looking after someone who has depression is incredibly hard work and it takes a toll on your own mental health. Share how you feel with other people and be open about it. Be realistic about what you can achieve in helping to make them better. If the older person you care for is depressed and apathetic, it might put pressure on you to do more for them because they don't have the energy to do things for themselves. Try to get others to support you in encouraging them to continue to do as much as possible. There will be occasions when you feel desperate and miserable and spend more time thinking about their health rather than your own. There is more about this in Chapter Five.

Find positives where you can and make sure to explore all possibilities of taking a break. Look at Chapter Three to find out whether there are any financial supports or benefits that can help you to pay for replacement care, travel costs or respite, and look at Useful Contacts and Resources.

Three hints

1. Your health must come first; you can't help if you are unwell
2. Caring for depression requires help
3. Registering as the carer and getting power of attorney reduces stress

Distressed behaviour

If the person you are caring for has dementia, from time to time they will display behaviour that is a result of distress. That distress may be caused by noise or other disturbance. It may be that they are in pain or that they're lonely or unhappy for some reason that you have yet to discover. This behaviour can present as aggression, agitation or anxiety. It makes life very difficult for carers, and that's why it is sometimes called disturbing behaviour.

When my mother was in the first care home, she used to bang on the windows and doors, night and day, shouting to be let out. They tried to stop her, but nothing seemed to work and they asked her to leave. At the next care home that behaviour stopped. The staff knew how to keep a calm environment and how to distract her. (Davina, daughter of Irene, 67 with Young Onset dementia)

The care workers took the trouble to find out all about Irene. They discovered that before she went to stay in the care home she was a keen gardener and hill walker and spent time outside no matter the weather. They devised a routine of getting her into outdoor clothes and shoes immediately after breakfast and taking her out for a walk until she was tired and wanted to come back for a cup of tea and a rest in the chair. Later in the day, if she was trying to leave, a quick turn around the garden was usually enough, or she could sit out there if the weather was good enough. In season, they encouraged her to work in their greenhouse, sowing seeds in pots or planting out. The distressed and distressing behaviour was a result of feeling trapped. The first home tried to reduce the behaviour by getting her to sit quietly and considering sedation. It was good that Irene 'escaped' that setting.

When you are faced with these problems at home you need to reach for help. There are addresses of websites where advice is given in Useful Contacts and Resources. There you will find ideas for keeping a calm environment. In some care settings the staff use sedatives prescribed by the doctor to control this kind of behaviour. This is not ideal because it can give rise to sleepiness that causes falls and injuries. Training is now given for staff to help them understand how they can, through activities and environmental changes, reduce distressed behaviour. There is no room to outline all of these here in this section, but you will find lots of ideas on the website of the **Dementia Services Development Trust**, which also gives information about some helpful literature. There is also useful information on my website www. juneandrews.net You can use the enquiries form on that website for specific problems.

This kind of behaviour is exhausting for the carer, and if there is any aggression then it's very important to remove yourself from danger. Don't try to restrain the person because both of you may become injured in the process. In all the advice given about how to deal with it, the most common solution is to provide the person with plenty of exercise and give them lots of attention to prevent them becoming bored. Exercise seems to help people calm down, and maybe a friend can help by regularly taking them for a walk. You do need to discuss this with the doctor, or the community psychiatric nurse if you have one.

Three hints

1. Distressed behaviour is common
2. You can prevent, reduce or stop it if you know the cause
3. Get help from clinical staff and ideas from websites

Doctors

The Royal College of General Practitioners has noted that nine out of ten carers visit their local GP surgery every year, but many of them do not say they are carers. You must let your GP know that you are a carer and make sure that it is put in your own medical records. They can use other methods to discover you, but why would you not help? Many practices have at least one member who leads on carers' issues. They might be administrative or clinical, but they are the source of information. They have a register which they use to call in carers for flu jabs or health checks and to send out newsletters or information about relevant events in the local area. They recognise the value of engaging with carers. There might be a poster in the waiting room advertising this.

Some doctors have a carer pack that they give to carers which includes:

- A letter informing you of the benefits they offer carers, such as the flu jab.
- A letter to the patient asking them to consent to you accessing relevant medical information.

- A carer's leaflet.
- A list of your local carer organisations and other health agencies and resources.
- Past newsletters for carers from the practice or a local organisation.

The doctor will be able to help you by writing letters about issues such as the Blue Badge scheme and Attendance Allowance. In addition, ask the district nurse if they can support you by putting you in touch with other services and letting you know what is available in your local area. Your GP will find it hard to keep up to date with local carer support services, or carer breaks and grants, but they can let you know about local carer organisations who should be more up to date.

When they know about you, the family doctor can be more flexible about home visits and give you double appointments when you can talk to them about your own health and then they can talk to the person you are caring for about their health. Of course, that only works if you both have the same GP. It saves you having to make double journeys. But even if you have the same GP, things can go wrong.

I know what dementia looks like because both my mother and father had it. Now I can see it in my husband. He refuses to go to see our GP. Even though I have welfare power of attorney I can't make him. He's paranoid and getting hostile and my life is a misery. Because he won't get a diagnosis, I can't be seen as his carer and none of those benefits that I've read about can be given to me. I'm completely stuck. (Geraldine, 79)

GPs are much more receptive these days to spotting dementia and supporting dementia carers. However, they do get tangled up in ideas of patient confidentiality and become quite secretive.

They keep telling me about his rights, but what about mine?
(Geraldine, 79)

In a case like this, Geraldine may be able to get help from a local Alzheimer organisation, who will have met this sort of situation before and may know of sympathetic clinicians who will be able to help a carer in these circumstances.

Three hints

1. Get registered as a carer with the GP
2. Make sure you have got consent to share medical information
3. Most doctors are great, but you can ask to see another.

Dying

Caring for someone who is dying at home is a demanding experience, both physically and emotionally. You should expect support from your GP and the district nurses. It may be that a charity such as **Macmillan** or **Marie Curie** is able to provide nurses and carers at night to allow you to get sleep.

People sometimes wonder what the final days will be like if they have never been with a dying person before. In the time before people die, they typically sleep a lot and rest. The various body systems are just quietly shutting down. They probably won't eat or drink much, if anything.

The health care team can set up home care services to give you help with the care. Not least, the palliative care team can make sure that the person you are caring for does not suffer any pain. Don't hesitate to ask them for more pain relief if you think that it's not working.

You need to be aware of your limits and know when to ask for help to provide the best care. You may wish to be with the person all the time, but you yourself must rest. District nurses can support you with advice and assistance in practical aspects, for example how to care for someone who is spending all the time in bed. They may provide special equipment such as air mattresses that will keep the person comfortable.

The person may have asked to die at home, and although you're trying to make sure this happens, it might not be possible for you. You may consider asking for a transfer to a **hospice**. It's not a failure when that happens. Everyone has to adapt to circumstances. Remember to ask friends and family for support. Even if all they can do is bring you food or make phone calls, it will make a difference. Tell them what would help. You need a listening ear, and if you are a member of a faith community they will know what they can do to support you.

There is more about what to expect in Chapter Six. The advice here relates to when you are nursing someone at home. Very many people die at home or in a care home, and there is much more on this in that chapter, including information about legal and administrative things you have to do.

Three hints

1. There are health care teams who can support you to allow a death at home
2. Pain is not necessary
3. Your friends can help and don't hesitate to tell them what you need

Eating well

You will see more information about this under the heading 'Cooking'. For older people, eating well depends on a range of things including their health, any medication that they must take, any problems with teeth or swallowing that affect what they can have, and other underlying issues.

To find out what the person should eat, get help from a dietician. They are available in hospitals, and community dieticians can help in care homes or at home. A lot will depend on how big an appetite the person has. In older people the appetite is often small, and they will require encouragement or even supplements.

It's important to emphasise the benefit of fibre because constipation is something that can make life miserable and uncomfortable. It also leads to confusion and illness in very old people. At a time of life when opportunities for fun may be limited, people should be allowed to self-indulge a bit, and so they might not want to stick to one of those healthy Mediterranean diets. Keeping up fluid intake is important, and you can help with that by making sure that all the things that would encourage drinking, such as the teapot and jugs of water, are clearly visible and the person can help themselves. Leaving a flask of tea handy can make things easier.

Eating in company can make the person who has not been eating enough more likely to take in more food. Eating is an intensely social activity.

When I would offer a cake to my granny, she would refuse it even if I encouraged her. A few moments later, when she saw everybody else was taking one, she would then take one for herself. In encouraging her to eat I ended up putting on weight. Because I had to eat to keep her company! Another trick was to order a side order of chips for myself when we went to a café. I would then say that I didn't have room for them, and she would quickly eat them up with ketchup because she couldn't bear the thought of me 'wasting' perfectly good food. (Ailidh, 23)

You can buy crockery and cutlery that helps people with sensory and physical impairments to eat and drink independently. You will find ideas on the **AskSARA** website or from an occupational therapist (see contact details in Useful Contacts and Resources). Start with establishing the best place to sit up while eating, and the ideal position of the plate, cup and cutlery. Non-slip place mats help stabilise the plates, and plates with a raised edge can prevent food spilling while the person is scooping it up. Angled spoons and forks are great if the person has restricted movement in their shoulder or arm. You can buy an electronic stabilising handle for cups, and attachments that will stabilise a spoon or fork if the person has a marked tremor that makes it hard to eat independently. There are major advances in automated eating devices, and though some of them are hugely expensive they can be rented or leased and may sometimes be provided by the local authority.

Appetite will be stimulated by attractive smells. The right aroma can increase the appetite in people who do not think they are hungry, even if the person does not notice the smell. You can buy a device that will release authentic food fragrances in the living space, which gets the gastric juices flowing, so the person will anticipate and welcome food. The smell of chocolate, coffee or hot apple pie is used commercially to increase trade in shops and restaurants. Essential oils work in a diffuser machine, just like a domestic air freshener you might use at home to cover other smells. If someone has a poor appetite, being around delicious smells coming from the hob or oven and helping with preparations in the kitchen can tempt them to try what you've been cooking.

Three hints

1. Eating alone is hard for some people

2. The mechanics of eating can be helped with special cutlery
3. The smell of cooking can improve anyone's appetite

Emergency plan

This is a plan that you set out so that care can be provided in case of emergencies. You may find a blank **emergency planning template** on the website of carer organisations, for example www. actionforcarers.org.uk.

Planning ahead makes a sudden change of circumstances less likely to create a crisis. In the plan you record general information about the person and their contact details, and the name of anyone who holds a key for the house where they stay. Make sure all the people involved know that they are named on it. There are spaces for contact details of people who can be reached if you're not available, and information about any provider agencies that normally go into the house. If someone has power of attorney or lasting power of attorney, then the details should be there as well. Contacts for the GP and the pharmacy are needed in case there is a medical emergency. There is much more information that can be included, and you can decide what is most important. Copies of it should be given to those mentioned and to care agencies, and one copy left with the person you care for.

The plan can be set out like a daily diary, with the routine of times and tasks and who is expected to call in. It should be a live document that is updated regularly and provides the information needed for the first two or three days after an emergency that prevents you from providing your usual care. Special information in the plan would include where medication is kept, information on any allergies, and anything else that the person who steps in for you should know. The time to do it is now.

The emergency plan is different from the **Bottle in the Fridge** emergency information scheme. These bottles are for older people who live in their own homes and have health issues. Basic medical information is put inside a special bottle that is stored in the fridge. Service providers will know this is a good place to look for essential information in an emergency, and they are alerted to this by a sticker just inside the front door, which tells them to look in the fridge. That information is brief, but essential. You could have both an emergency plan and a fridge bottle and one could refer to the other.

Three hints

1. Get a plan template before you think you might need it
2. Involve others in making the plan
3. Make sure that key people know there is a plan and where to find it

Equipment for household tasks

The **Disabled Living Foundation** has produced a website called **AskSARA** with over ninety topics to choose from. There are local versions of AskSARA over most of the country, so check for the one in your area. It would be impossible in a book like this to begin to list the sort of equipment and advice that is available. So the best we can do is provide the web address and recommend that you have a look to see what is there that you didn't know you needed. asksara.livingmadeeasy.org.uk

Your local area may have a **Disabled Living Centre** (**DLC**), where you can get free and impartial information and advice about equipment which can help people who have difficulties with normal activities. You can see and try out equipment. This might include chairs, stairlifts, kitchen and bathroom equipment, powered wheelchairs and scooters, and equipment that supports walking. There should be an occupational therapist or therapy assistant there with a wide range of knowledge to help you find what you need. See the section on Home Adaptations on p. 189 for more information.

Three hints

1. You can be provided with, hire or buy most things
2. Looking at a website is a start, but seeing the kit is better
3. Advice from an occupational therapist is valuable

Falls prevention

Much of this advice about falls prevention is repeated in the section on 'Home adaptations'. Removing clutter and frayed carpets and getting rid of scatter rugs is a good start. If there must be rugs, attach them to the floor so that they cannot slip using double-sided carpet tape or gripper tape. If the rug is over fitted carpet, you can use rug pins to secure it to the underlying carpet.

Mop up spillages on hard floors. Apply a non-skid treatment to the floor. There are products specifically for wood floors. The transition from one type of floor type to another is a risky threshold. People with neurological conditions or visual impairment misperceive it as a step and may stumble. An example might be where the hall carpet ends and the bathroom floor starts.

No matter what the floors are like, well-fitting shoes are important to prevent falls. It is a bad idea to walk about in socks. Floppy slippers are even worse.

One Christmas the Brownies held a slipper amnesty where all the old people were able to bring in a used pair of slippers and they were confiscated so that the person could be issued with a brand-new pair of properly fitted slippers. This was part of a campaign to reduce falls in older people. (Elizabeth, Brownie leader)

Ask for a medication review to see if anything is being taken that would increase the fall risk. Some sedatives and antidepressants have that effect. Any medications that affect your brain, your blood pressure or your blood sugar can cause dizziness. Give the doctor details of any previous falls or near-misses. It is worth keeping a diary of those. The doctor will ask the patient about any joint pain, shortness of breath or numbness in the feet and legs when they walk. They might then refer them to the local Falls Prevention Service.

After a fall people sometimes lose confidence and take less exercise, which is a bad idea because decreasing exercise can increase the risk of a fall. You want to do things that will improve your balance, flexibility, muscle strength and gait. Walking is a very good exercise for this, and it helps your mental health too. As a carer you may find it useful to recruit a buddy who will take your person out for a walk regularly. That gives you some respite while making them less likely to fall over.

Three hints

1. An exercise programme improves strength and balance
2. Review medicines and glasses
3. Safety-check the home

Finance

Chapter Three covers money advice for carers. It is well known from research and experience that carers suffer financial hardship because of their caring work, and some of the solutions that are presented to the other practical problems in this chapter do require money. Look at Chapter Three to see if there are any ways of generating the resources you need to implement the practical solutions that will make your life as a carer easier. The websites listed there with benefits calculators should help you work out what you are entitled to, and some of the charities listed in Useful Contacts and Resources will be able to assist you in making the application. Be realistic about how much caring is costing you.

My sister visits Dad, who is twenty miles away, two or three times a week by car. She brings him some food from her home, and sometimes brings washing away with her to do for next time. When I ask her, she says she doesn't need any recompense and Dad doesn't need to claim any allowances. (Eleanor)

If Eleanor's sister was a business, she'd be claiming 45p per mile from the taxman for her journeys. She might not notice the cost of the food she is bringing, but it is hard to make a meal for someone for less than £3. A service wash costs easily £15. If you add it up, that's getting close to £100 per week without counting her time. She needs to think about how much all this is costing her.

Money is often at the root of conflict between sibling carers. Having an open adult conversation about it is not always easy.

We hate each other and we have always done, so why would we have a collaborative conversation now about the cost of looking after our mother? (Dolores, talking about her brother Keith)

Dolores was providing most of the care for their mother in the last three years of her life. Keith had little to do with either of them until the last few months. When their mother died, her will split everything she had equally between her two children. Dolores felt cheated, because Keith got the same as her and she had spent a fortune. She knew her mother intended to treat them equally and asked Keith if he would repay her some of that expense from his half of the legacy. They just fell out and never spoke to each other again. Dolores is sorry that she did not support her mother to claim things she was entitled to because, in effect, she ended up preserving her brother's legacy and subsidising every other taxpayer in the land.

Three hints

1. Register as a carer
2. Seriously think about how much this is costing and talk to your family
3. Get information about what you and the person you care for are entitled to

First aid responses

Choking

I hope you're not looking this up while something is currently going wrong. The time to know about first aid is long before the emergency takes place. Because choking is such a significant issue it is covered in a separate heading here. To save you looking that up, the answer is **Heimlich Manoeuvre** (p. 158).

Falls

The most common accident is a fall. When someone falls you may have the urge to get them back up on their feet quickly. First check if they are conscious and breathing normally, and if not call for help (999) and start CPR (Cardiopulmonary Resuscitation) if you know how to do it. If you don't, the call handler will talk you through it. It's not for me to tell you here.

If they are conscious and responding to you, try to get them to talk by asking questions about how they are. This helps you work out if they've perhaps had a stroke or a fit, which would also alert you to call for help. Don't move them if they are injured. Stop any bleeding with some pressure on a pad. Serious signs would be trouble breathing, a headache, sudden sleepiness and bruises that get larger and more painful.

If there is nothing obviously or seriously wrong they might be able to get themselves back up, for example if you bring a chair over for them to pull themselves up on. They can roll over on to hands and knees and get up slowly. If they are heavy and unable to get up alone, don't try to help because you might hurt yourself and that helps no one. Keep them warm with a blanket and cushions and call for an ambulance. Some ambulance services will lend a device to help get a person off the floor, which means they don't get frequent calls from the same household. They will probably refer you to a **falls prevention service**. Sometimes they take the person to hospital, but not always.

Seizures

An older person may experience a seizure for the first time. Dial 999 if it is the first seizure, if it lasts longer than five minutes, if another seizure starts straight after the first, if breathing is difficult after the seizure stops, or if they are injured. The person may have convulsions, a fall, a blackout, may wander or lose the ability to speak. Sometimes the older person just slumps over on their seat, appearing unconscious and apparently losing bladder control. Ease them into the recovery position and turn them to one side so any fluids drain away from the mouth. Don't hold them down or put anything in their mouth.

Later, if you are living with an older person with seizures who has other medical problems, check with the doctor about how they want you to respond when a seizure happens. Ask whether or when you should call an ambulance and if there are any special warning signals that you should be on the lookout for. Checking the time and the length of the seizure and keeping a note is useful so that you can pass on this information.

There is training about this on the website of the Epilepsy Society www.epilepsysociety.org.uk

Three hints
1. Take any training on offer
2. Don't hurt yourself while caring for someone on the floor
3. Check out the issues with doctors afterwards, even if things look OK

Frailty

The word frailty is used a lot about older people. When you say that someone looks frail, it ordinarily means that they look weak and delicate. In fact, the current guidance from the National Institute for Clinical Excellence (NICE) says that whenever an older person goes to hospital, doctors should identify frailty and grade it. It is not an illness but a combination of natural ageing, loss of fitness and, for some, the effects of several long-term conditions. The person is often tired, with unintended weight loss and reduced strength. Their ability to get over an illness or injury is greatly reduced, so a minor incident can reduce the quality or length of their life. That means they might not benefit from some major interventions like cardiac resuscitation. Because of that a frail person may decide that they do not want doctors to attempt resuscitation if they collapse. This is often referred to as a **DNR** or **DNAR order** (Do Not Attempt Resuscitation). Best practice requires that such orders are discussed with the family. The discussion should be kept up to date.

The assessment which in hospitals is often done using the **Rockwood Clinical Frailty Scale** is not about how they are when they are admitted to hospital, but about how the person is normally. The aim in hospital is to get them back to that previous state. It is important to let the staff know how this person was two weeks ago. That should be the baseline. Professor Kenneth Rockwood is a world-leading doctor in this field, and he talks about the difference between an 80-year-old who can run a marathon and another 80-year-old who cannot get out of bed. He points out that as humans we have evolved higher-level functions. This includes walking upright, being able to exercise vigorously and having divided attention. He says, 'When those things fail, we can't think properly, we can't function properly, we can't move properly, we are at risk of falls.' You can find this scale easily on the internet and spot which level the older person you care for is currently at.

Three hints

1. Frailty is common but varies a lot
2. Know your person's level of frailty and tell the clinicians
3. Realise that frailty sometimes leads to poorer outcomes, and be prepared

Friends

Friendships built up over a long time are like money in your purse. At times you have enough to give away, and at other times you might need to accept some. But for some people, the traditional saying about it being 'better to give than receive' has hardened into a notion that they don't want to be on the receiving end of help from anybody. It's a matter of pride.

There can be a problem when friends offer help that you don't need. They mean well, but they offer to do things that you'd rather do yourself. It is really important to learn how to say, 'You are so lovely. Thank you for offering to do X. What I really need is someone who could do Y for me. Is there any chance you could do that instead?' This is twice as hard because you are saying no to an offer and making a demand. Rest assured that a true friend only wants to help, and the clue you give them about what would make a difference is vital for them and for you.

Friends are not a luxury. They are a necessity for maintaining your health and sanity. You need friends in order to be happy, and you need to tell them that you need them. Just remember to give them specific jobs. And if you are a friend, remember to ask what is needed. Food is always good.

Three hints

1. Friends are a necessity, not a luxury
2. It is sometimes better to receive than to give
3. Don't underestimate the power of a casserole

Herbert Protocol

This is a national scheme encouraging carers to provide helpful information to the police which can be used if a vulnerable person goes missing. It is often applied when people are living with dementia. It is useful even if you have gone to the trouble of buying or renting a locator device, because sometimes people have left their locator device at home when they go missing. You don't know where they are and that's the definition of missing. There is more about this under the heading 'Wandering'. The protocol may be part of your emergency plan. You must register for the scheme, but it has great advantages for reducing your stress and saving police time if it gets to the point of searching for someone. The longer you wait before calling for help, the further the lost person will have gone, and the chance of finding them happy and well has diminished.

If you Google 'The Herbert Protocol' you will find out if the scheme has been introduced by your own police force, for example Police Scotland, West Yorkshire Police, Derbyshire Constabulary, etc. All the information is there. It will ask you to fill out a form to capture what is useful.

Three hints

1. Have an emergency plan
2. The first time somebody becomes lost, join the national scheme
3. Don't hesitate to call for help

Home adaptations

Advice on design adaptations in the home is based on understanding the normal changes of ageing, and what can be done to compensate for them. A lot of housing is poorly designed and requires adaptations and aids to be put in place if someone living there has a sensory, cognitive or physical impairment or disability. One day all housing will be universally designed in a way that accommodates people for the whole of their lives. But in the meantime, it's good to know what changes can be made that are affordable and will make a difference. You can start making these changes to your own home now in preparation for later life.

The reaction times of older people are reduced, increasing the likelihood of injury from slips or trips. Younger people can recover their balance if they stumble. For older people the consequences of a fall are much more serious. It can be the first step towards hospitalisation, on the way to residential care. There are obvious changes that you can make, including putting non-slip strips in the bath and shower and coating hard floors with non-slip wax. Installing a wet room and making sure that there is a non-slip waterproof seat in the shower makes bathing safer.

Increasing the light level at home makes a huge difference because there are changes in the ageing eye which have the same effect as wearing sunglasses inside the house. Or yellow goggles. Maximise the natural light by opening curtains and blinds and increase the number of lamps or the brightness of lamps in the rooms. It goes without saying that making sure the person has the right spectacles can help, and try to avoid glasses that go dark in sunlight because when coming into the house out of daylight the person is temporarily blinded and may fall over an unexpected obstacle.

Get an occupational therapist to come and do a risk assessment of the rooms, and they will certainly recommend that you remove rugs that might be a trip hazard and generally reduce clutter. Reducing clutter in wardrobes and cupboards can make it easier and less tiring for people to find things by themselves. Replacing standard knobs on doors with lever handles and doing the same with taps in the kitchen and bathroom helps people to use them independently if they have weakness in their hand or wrist.

Make sure there are non-slip treads on steps and put a bannister on stairways. Add a handrail on both sides. It would be ideal to have a toilet on the same floor as the bedroom for night-time and the living room for daytime. Who designs houses without that? Not carers.

People ask me what the secret is for my old age, and I tell them that it is taking time and holding the rail when you're going up and down the stairs. (Betty, 96)

It would help to have zero threshold entry points, including a walk-in bath and shower, but these changes start to be more expensive, as does widening doors and hallways and installing a stairlift. A well-designed house would already have light switches and electrical sockets on the walls at a level that could be accessed by a person sitting in a wheelchair.

These days, ordinary DIY stores sell kitchen units with accessible cupboards, like a pull-out pantry so you can reach items that would otherwise require stretching to the back of the cupboard, eye-level ovens and fridges, and cupboards with shelves that pull down, so people are less tempted to stand on a stool to reach up.

Dad stands on the kitchen worktop to change the time of the clock twice a year. He had done that for a couple of years before it crossed my mind to move the clock to a different place. Some changes are so obvious you just don't think of them. (Ellen, daughter of Alf)

Kitchen worktops and even sinks can be fitted that move up and down, so they can be used at sitting height for some people and altered for use when someone stands to use them.

My mum has tripped before now when rushing to answer the phone. We reduce that risk by having a phone in every room including her bedroom. I tried to tell her that if the call is important the person will ring back or leave a message, but she doesn't seem to really believe that. (Fiona, daughter of Enid, 76)

You can't change someone's personality! However, you might have more success when considering security devices for the home. Smart ideas for door locks include ones that are operated by fingerprints, and key safes are very common.

Three hints

1. Safety first
2. Design for old age while you are young
3. There are changes that are expensive, cheaper and cheap. Do what you can.

Hospice

Palliative care, or end-of-life care, aims to support the person to live as well as possible until they die. You as a carer also need support at this time. There are hard questions about what you might expect, and what available medical options might be offered by the doctors. Hospice staff, including nurses, can support you in advance or during those difficult conversations.

When people think about hospice care, they often associate it with cancer care at the end of life in a building specially provided and staffed for this specialist care. There may not be a building like that, and it might be that the staff come to where the person lives. Usually, hospice care is limited to the last six months of life. But it is not limited to cancer care. Increasingly, hospice care has a focus on all end-of-life care, including dementia. People don't often think of dementia as a life-limiting illness, but it is.

If you are caring for a person with dementia who is nearing the end of their life, it is hard to provide emotional and spiritual comfort. The person may be unresponsive, and you may be worn out after a long spell of caring. This is where hospice care can help you. The person you care for may not need to move away from home to receive this care, if hospice care can be provided at home.

Social services can provide equipment, and through the GP community nurses or nurses from Macmillan or Marie Curie may be able to come and help. If the person who is dying is in a care home or nursing home, it might be that they would prefer to stay there rather than move to another place such as an acute hospital.

The care provided in a hospice is free. Like a good care home, it extends to supporting people who are close to the person even after the death, during the bereavement period. It's important to be supported after the death of a loved one.

The Alzheimer's Society has a useful fact sheet on end-of-life care for people with dementia: www.alzheimers.org.uk/get-support/help-dementia-care/end-life-care-dementia

Three hints

1. Plan for the end of life; planning doesn't hasten it, but can make it more comfortable
2. Important conversations might be difficult, but hospice staff can help you to have them
3. Find your nearest hospice and talk to them well before it is necessary

Hospitals

Being a carer for someone in hospital became much more difficult during the pandemic over recent times. What became clear was that, in the absence of support from family and friends to visit, the experience of hospital was extremely difficult.

The advice given here is based on how things would be in normal times when visiting is free. Over recent years it has become easier to visit friends in hospital. Largely because of the John's Campaign, it has been made clear that visitors have a positive contribution to make especially when the patient is older and confused because of delirium or dementia.

> *Over 1,500 hospitals and homes (and some others, such as ambulance trusts, clinical commissioning participants, domiciliary care companies, hospices and primary care providers) have pledged to support our principles of inclusion. We believe that people, particularly those with dementia, other mental illnesses, or otherwise in need of care, should not be separated from those important to them by protocols and systems that are harmful and wrong. (johnscampaign.org.uk)*

Just as the NHS has always understood the importance of parents for children in hospital, so we now understand the importance to carers of always having access to their older friend or relative during a hospital stay. The family or other carers know the patient and can interpret what they are saying or explain whether there have been any recent changes in their behaviour. The carer also knows from non-verbal behaviour what the person is communicating when it doesn't make sense to anybody else. Their outcome is hugely influenced by this contact. Visiting was always open for children, but now it has been extended to older people.

A lot of the advice in this book has been about avoiding hospital admission. Sometimes you can't avoid it. What do you do then?

Emergency department

The hospital admission often starts in the emergency department. Try to stay with the person for as long as possible to help with answering questions and to keep them cheerful. Patients can be waiting in the emergency department for a long time before a hospital bed is available, and if allowed you may be able to make sure that the person has something to eat or drink. You can even help them to use the toilet. The nursing staff are very busy with emergencies and so your help will be appreciated. It is a very noisy place, so if you're able to supply headphones with some familiar music or a story it can help distract the person from what's making them ill and from the chaos round about them.

In the ward

Once they have been admitted to the ward, it will help the patient to settle in if they have some familiar things with them. Gifts of flowers are no longer allowed in clinical settings but bringing magazines, photos and cards for people to look at has two purposes. It gives them something to do when you are not there, but also it signals to those caring for them that they do have friends and family. These materials can be a topic of conversation even when you are not there.

Jo-jo, the ward domestic, used to pretend to be annoyed when the cards fell off the locker on to the floor. 'You're making my ward untidy,' he'd say. 'Who else has been writing to you?' and he'd listen to the lady talking about her grandchildren while he got on with mopping and dusting. (Hospital visitor)

Eating and drinking

There is always a danger that a person in hospital will become dehydrated. Staff are very much more aware of this these days, but it's still the case that the person might be asleep for a long time and not think to drink water when they wake up. Dehydration can make an older person confused or increase underlying confusion that already exists. When you are visiting, do everything you can to encourage the person to drink.

Eating the right things is an important part of getting well, and in response to this hospitals have introduced protected mealtimes. This means that patients are protected from visits from staff or examinations during the time when they should be eating. Usually visitors are also excluded during this time, but you can make a special case to come in and help the person you care for to eat their meal. Sometimes, if they do not eat the food it is taken away. In hospital you are expected to eat at mealtimes so there is limited availability of food in between. When you are visiting you may be able to remedy that.

Pain relief

There is no need to suffer pain. In hospital the nurses will come round at regular intervals and offer medication. They give medication that has been prescribed for that time. However, in between times they can usually offer extra for 'breakthrough' pain. Very many older people do not like to disturb the nurse and ask for it. Or, if they're asked by the nurse, they will say that they are fine because they think it is bad to take too many medicines. Sometimes the nursing staff will have to be persuaded or reminded that the patient is uncomfortable even though the patient is not prepared to admit it. If you're visiting, you can help with this. Because you know the person, you may realise that they're in pain when no one else notices it. If staff seem hesitant to provide pain relief you can certainly ask why.

Confusion and agitation

An older person in hospital may appear confused and agitated at times. It is vital for the care staff to understand whether this is normal for them or something new that has happened since they came to hospital. The causes can include urine infection or chest infection, and sometimes it is a question of dehydration, lack of sleep or stress from the unfamiliar surroundings. When a patient is ill like this it may be that they now have delirium (see 'Delirium' in this chapter). This is a clinical condition which requires treatment including hydration and oxygen, and removal of the underlying causal factors.

The agitated patient who cries out and walks around can cause huge stress for other patients, so there is a danger that they will be sedated in the interest of their neighbours. This sedation might not be in the interest of your older relative, however, and a solution such as finding a single room would be better for their health. Talk to the staff if you think this form of chemical restraint is being used. It might still be concluded that this is the only option, but it should be discussed with all concerned.

When we visited the ward in the early evening, everyone was asleep. My colleague thought this was peaceful, but I was deeply suspicious. Some should be sleeping, but not everyone at the same time. (Hospital visitor)

Helpful things to do

There is a long list of useful things that you can do when visiting. If busy staff don't have time to let the patient do things slowly, such as washing and dressing, you could offer to help. Find ways of having open visiting. Make rotas with friends and family to make sure the person has someone with them as much as possible. Take the person for some exercise and get them into daylight if you can. Have a memory book or communications passport that allows their likes and dislikes to be recorded. Check ankles for swelling and encourage them to put their feet up. Take them to the toilet and wash their hands. Wash their face. Find a way of letting staff know 'who' is in the bed. Try to get the staff to see you as an extra pair of hands, but also don't hesitate to challenge if you spot things you don't like, such as reddened skin where the person has been sitting too long, or meaningless loud music and chatter that no one is listening to from a TV that no one can see.

Leaving the hospital

Frail older people may be offered a 'home visit' to see if they are well enough to go home. This happens if the staff have doubts. Sometimes the person is nudged towards care-home care without trying to get them home with support first. You may have to fight for this, and you might be doing it against the clock because of the pressure to free up beds. If your relative is in a clinical setting that is not good there is not much you can do to improve the hospital, but your presence can improve or modify the behaviour of some of the staff and the patient's progress through the system. Sometimes when things go wrong it is not from carelessness, but not knowing what is needed. Don't hesitate to make it clear to them.

Three hints

1. Think about hydration and pain
2. Use visiting times to make a practical difference
3. Support the staff, but challenge them when needed

Liaising with care services

Sometimes being a carer, even if it is at long distance, is like being a 'project worker' in a complex undertaking. I don't say 'project manager', because at times what happens is out of your control. You are already having to read this book for information, and even though it tries to put everything in one place, it must refer you to websites because local variation is huge and rules and regulations change all the time. Making appointments, arranging transport, ensuring supplies of medicines ... everything takes time and there are so many things to do. It is even worse when things go wrong.

If there is a problem, you should keep a diary of issues and keep notes of phone calls and meetings. You really need a file for this. Always put any complaints in writing. There can be problems with the quality of personal care, or other needs not being met. You may know stories of carers having to stay off work because the care workers funded by the agency or council did not turn up.

Managing care workers who come in and out of the house can be difficult. If an agency has a problem with staffing, you may get a call at very short notice to say that no one is coming. Agencies should have a back-up plan in case of an emergency, but this doesn't always happen. You will have to make a formal complaint. If the local authority is funding the care, you can complain to them. If you are funding it, you need to speak to the agency manager to give them a chance to investigate, explain and put things right. The manager may not even know that this happened until you tell them. You can take your complaint higher, eventually to the Ombudsman. Their details are in the Useful Contacts and Resources chapter. In Scotland the regulator will investigate individual complaints, but not in the rest of the UK.

Some of your problems can arise from the person you care for not wanting to have care workers in the house. Also, siblings who are not providing direct care might support the older person who is refusing outside help. Families need to work together on this.

Because I had provided so much of the direct care for Mum, I thought that when she started to have care workers my life would be simpler. But that's far from the truth. There were constant spats when she would send them away. I spent so much time negotiating with the manager and liaising with them, it almost felt as if it would've been easier just to do it myself. But of course that was not feasible. It was interesting that my brother started to imagine that my life was stress-free with having the care workers, so I had to put him right on that. But it was still worth having the extra support. (Lesley, daughter of Grace, 84)

If you do not live in the same house, or if you cannot visit frequently because you are in another part of the country, you can ask the agency to send you a monthly report. If you are in the house, you can look at the report sheets that are filled out by care workers to see if what should be happening is evidenced in the records. The person you care for may be able to tell you about any problems themselves. If they are not happy, or have an aversion to a particular carer, this gives you a clue. However, the person you care for may be impossible to please, so it's not simple.

Three hints

1. You cannot assume that care workers will always do what they are supposed to do
2. If there are problems, there are ways of complaining and getting them fixed
3. The best clue is whether the person cared for is happy, even though some people seem never to be happy

Managing finances

There is detail about this in Chapter Three. Finance includes helping the person manage their own affairs, but also eventually managing them for the person. It is made much easier if you have **power of attorney**, which is also discussed in that chapter and in the essential book *Power of Attorney: The One-Stop Guide*.

Three hints

1. It's never too soon to sort powers of attorney for yourself
2. Nor for the older person you care for to get themselves an attorney
3. Finance is difficult; read Chapter Three

Medicines

Often older people in need of care have been prescribed many medicines. You might not be confident that the person you care for understands their medicines and is good at taking the right dose at the right time. You can ask the local pharmacist, or a pharmacist based at the GP practice, to do a structured medication review. 'Polypharmacy' is the word used to describe the situation when someone is taking too many medicines. The combined side-effects of these medications are sometimes put down to ageing. But the tiredness, constipation, loss of appetite, confusion, falls and many other symptoms may actually be the result of the pills that are being taken for some other reason. The pharmacist knows about how medicines can affect older people differently from younger people.

A rule of thumb is that an old person should not be taking any more than five different drugs. Remember that they may also be self-medicating with over-the-counter medicines that they have picked up from the pharmacy or supermarket. 'De-prescribing' is the word used for going through that list of medicines and making sure anything that's not needed is stopped, and anything which is reacting badly with another medicine is replaced. Sometimes people have been prescribed medicine for a symptom and they keep taking it even though it didn't make any difference, or the symptom has gone away on its own.

Pill organisers, also called dosette boxes or blister packs, help stop medicines being mixed up. These are boxes with a different compartment for each time of the day and each day of the week. They can be loaded by the carer or the person you are caring for, or come ready-packed from the pharmacy. This helps prevent common errors such as accidentally taking the medicine twice. If the person starts to forget to take medicine, you could ask for a care worker to give a prompt or get an automatic pill dispenser. Sometimes the pill dispenser has an alert that can warn you on your smartphone that the person has not taken their medication at the right time. There is more about this sort of kit on the AskSARA website (see Useful Contacts and Resources).

If the person is refusing to take their medicine, ask for advice from the pharmacist. For example, if they are having problems swallowing pills there might be an alternative syrup. Don't crush medicines without taking advice. Hiding their medicine disguised in food is a serious course of action because you are making someone do something without their consent. Ask the doctor if this medicine is essential for life before considering an action like that and make sure she knows that you are doing it. And because you already have enough to do, ask the pharmacy if they do a delivery service.

Three hints

1. Get a pharmacy review
2. Use a pill dispenser
3. Ask for delivery services

Mouth care

Dental symptoms are one of the most common calls to NHS111, the out-of-hours emergency doctor service, particularly at weekends. It used to be that people had lost all their teeth by the time they were 60. This is relatively rare now and has given rise to a specialist branch of dentistry for older people. Problems with eating and drinking can be caused by someone having a sore mouth, and so helping with mouth care has benefits other than avoiding pain. Some other health problems can arise from having infected gums. As well as tooth loss, there can be complications such as increasing the risk of stroke, diabetes and heart disease. Gum disease has even been linked to causation of dementia. There is a risk of getting respiratory infections if you breathe in bacteria from your mouth, causing pneumonia and other diseases. So keep that mouth nice and fresh.

Make sure there are regular visits to the dentist (or from the dentist. They will attend a care home). Brushing teeth twice daily and using a fluoride toothpaste will remove bacterial plaque and keep good hygiene. Remember to floss between the teeth and brush the tongue before brushing. Neglecting this can lead to bleeding gums and toothache. If there are dentures, they should be rinsed after food and cleaned every day, making sure they are not worn overnight.

There is more advice about dentistry on NHS Choices www.nhs. uk/live-well/healthy-body/take-care-of-your-teeth-and-gums/

Dentistry is one of the few NHS services where you have to pay a contribution to the cost. **The NHS Low Income Scheme (LIS)** may provide partial help with the cost of dental care for those who do not qualify for full help but still have a low income.

Three hints

1. Cleaning teeth reduces emergencies
2. See a dentist regularly
3. Check what could be free

Moving and handling

The most common injury for a carer is a back injury. When you hurt your back it can take a very long time to recover, and you may end up needing care yourself. The local council has an obligation to help carers avoid health and safety risks, so you should ask for a needs assessment for the person you look after as well as a carer's assessment for yourself. They might also offer free training courses on safe handling, or you could ask for a direct payment so you can pay for a course yourself (see Chapter Three). The council may provide free equipment such as hoists, stand aids, transfer boards or slide sheets to make moving someone safer and easier, and they should do a risk assessment for this kit. Advice from an occupational therapist or social worker should be sought before buying any equipment. You can get more information about what is available from the AskSARA website or a fact sheet from the **Disabled Living Foundation** at livingmadeeasy. org.uk/dlf-factsheets/choosing-a-hoist-and-slings-for-lifting-people. Further contact details are in Useful Contacts and Resources.

You may need to help someone get in or out of bed, turn over, sit up or in and out of a bath or chair. Bed rails and bath rails can help the person do a lot for themselves. The training will show you a checklist of things to think about before you try a lift. This includes considering whether they really do need help to move, or just supervision. How strong you are is important, as well as how heavy they are, and you should not attempt to lift a heavy weight without assistance. You need to check that the surface is not slippery and your shoes are right for this. Getting it wrong can injure the person you are caring for as well as yourself. Nobody needs that.

Three hints

1. Don't do it
2. Get the person to do as much as possible themselves
3. If you must lift or move the person, get training and equipment first

Pain

If the person you are caring for is suffering from acute or chronic pain you should ask for a pain assessment and work with the GP to find the best treatment. A common problem in pain management is the communication between the person in pain and their doctor or nurse. The clinician might not appreciate how much benefit the person would have from pain relief. Being assertive with professionals is part of your role. Remember that the pain might be in their mouth, and a dentist can help, or in their feet, so a podiatrist appointment could solve the problem. As the carer you know the person best, and if they're not able to speak you can recognise mood changes, agitation, distress or rapid breathing and frowning, which indicate that there is a problem. If they are immobile, the occupational therapist and physiotherapist may be able to help you with exercises or changes in seating arrangements or bed mattresses and wedges to make them more comfortable. It isn't necessary for anyone to suffer pain. As well as medication, emotional and spiritual support make a difference. Complementary therapy works for many people, and at the very least it offers a distraction and some comfort. Acupuncture, chiropractic services and massage can give relief. Use anything that works.

Three hints

1. Pain exists, even if the person can't define it well
2. Some clinicians need persuading to provide prescriptions
3. Try a wide range of physical, medicinal and emotional supports to get results

Registering as a carer

You should register with your GP that you are a carer, even if you love being a carer and don't mind what it costs you in time and money. There are still advantages you can get that money could not buy. If you need to prove that you are a carer you can use a Blue Badge letter or Carer's Allowance award letter. You are still a carer even when you don't have these if you give unpaid care to a family member, friend or neighbour who needs support. If you don't live in the same place as the person you care for, their local authority, rather than your own local authority, should assess your needs.

If you are not offered an assessment by the local authority you must ask for one. It is not only about your financial means. It is also about the amount of care you provide and how it affects your life and your health. There will also be consideration of planning for emergencies, including, in some areas, **carer emergency card schemes**. When help is urgently needed you might contact a family member, friend or neighbour who can cover, but it's not always possible. Carers are asked to register and with help from a skilled worker draw up an emergency plan. The plans are held by the scheme, which provides a twenty-four-hour response service. Carers carry a card with the scheme's telephone number and a unique ID number. Check with a local carer's organisation to see if such a scheme operates in your area. There is more about this in the Big List under 'Emergency plan'.

If you are reading this book you probably know you are a carer, but it is surprising how many people don't recognise that. If you don't claim the title you are cutting yourself off from a great deal of help and support for your friend or relative.

Three hints

1. Caring can be selfless, but there is no value in being invisible
2. Make sure their GP knows you
3. Have an emergency plan

Respite

Respite care is important for carers' well-being. Because caring can be so exhausting, it is natural for the carer to need a rest. Having an occasional break may be the thing that allows a carer to keep going for longer. Any short-term relief can be described as respite.

Respite might involve a regular afternoon or evening off, or an occasional period of days or weeks. The support that is given can be in the home of the person cared for, as when a friend comes round on a regular basis to free up the carer to go out and about. Temporary home care may be provided for a short time by an agency. Some care organisations can arrange live-in care for a few days or weeks to allow the carer to go away on holiday. For people with dementia or even mild cognitive impairment it is less disruptive to provide the respite care at home. A common alternative is a short stay in a residential home, which can be a step towards eventually going to live in that place if the person likes it.

There are also **day centres** where the older person can be cared for with other older people and a variety of activities are offered. You can find out about them from your local carer's organisation, social work or the GP. These services for older people are often described as if they are for the benefit of the attendee, but their chief value may be for giving the carer some free time. Therefore the transport arrangements are crucial. Depending on who organises it, the timing might not be very specific. You may have to organise transport yourself. It is impossible to plan your time off if you need to get the older person up and dressed and ready to leave by 9 a.m. 'in case' the transport arrives at the start of a two-hour window. The process of getting them out to the day care might undo the restfulness that was intended for the carer if the day begins with two hours of trying to reassure and explain what is going to happen next.

Some holiday providers can arrange a holiday setting with specialist support for the person with care needs to go on holiday with their carer. They may help with travel arrangements and provide opportunities for the carer to do things on their own by supplying local carers during the visit.

There are charitable organisations that support **short breaks for carers** listed at the end of the book. The local authority may agree to provide some support with this. Costs for care at home are at least the same if not more than the cost for staying in a care home. The benefit of the person being in their own environment is considerable. If there is a companion animal such as a dog, a live-in carer can help look after them, allowing the faithful pet to provide companionship while the family carer takes a little time to themselves.

The local authority social services team may suggest respite care during the care needs assessment.

Three hints

1. Carers need a rest
2. Some forms of respite cause more problems than they should

3. There might be local authority support, and a needs assessment will show that

Safeguarding

Protecting people who are at risk is known as 'safeguarding'. All local authorities have safeguarding policies. The aim is to support the person to live in safety, free from abuse and neglect.

I am the safeguarding lead and the sort of case I've looked into recently included one where an older lady seemed to be making unexplained withdrawals from her bank account. In another case there was poor care being provided by a home care agency in someone's house. There seemed to be neglect over a period of weeks and the lady was looking unwell, and obviously losing weight. In both cases it was not the lady who reported it, but a concerned neighbour. (Social worker)

Safeguarding enquiries should be made where a person who has need for care is experiencing or is at risk of abuse or neglect. You might report a service provider to safeguarding if you think the resident is not being supported and encouraged to make their own decisions, with informed consent. It could be that the care workers are failing to do their job properly. Care workers might raise a safeguarding issue if they are worried about the nature of the relationship between the person cared for and their carer and whether the carer is able to provide the necessary care or is neglecting the person or even abusing them.

It is not unknown for an elderly or vulnerable spouse to be abused by the person they are trying to care for and to suffer from self-neglect. Being isolated and not getting any practical or emotional support increases the risk of abuse of carers. So a carer can be the person who raises the concern, being vulnerable to harm or abuse, or they can be the abuser themselves. In circumstances where the carer has reached their limits, the safeguarding process can bring together a group of people representing health, social work, even police and other relevant bodies to decide what can be done to help and to keep the situation safe.

Mrs X was the carer for her husband, who had been diagnosed with dementia. The GP noticed that she had unexplained bruising and was generally anxious, especially in the presence of her husband. (Social worker)

Unintentional harm or neglect may be prevented by extra support, or it might be that other agencies should be involved to monitor the situation.

Three hints

1. Both carers and cared for may need support and protection
2. Local authorities must listen when concerns are raised
3. The solution may be more support, or replacing the carer with an agency

Self-directed support

There are lots of barriers to claiming allowances: stigma, not wanting to be described in the terms that are used on the forms, complications of the system, being turned down, negative people telling you there is no point, having to describe on paper the worst days of your life. All those things can put people off.

One complication is that there may be three different places from which funding is available. There could be some through the local authority social work department, some directly from central government, and some from the NHS. Most of it is a bureaucratic and administrative nightmare. Always reach out for help with the forms.

People who are eligible for social care support can by law get greater choice and control over how they receive these services through what is sometimes called the **self-directed support** approach. The systems have different names in Scotland and England because they come under different Acts of Parliament, but they amount to the same thing: after getting an assessment of care needs, someone from the local council's social care department will help to plan care. It's focused on what matters most to you (the outcomes) and ways of achieving that. It might be a mixture of what they call 'natural' support and 'funded' support. The council has a legal obligation to offer four options to people who have been assessed as needing a community care service. They must offer one of the following:

- A direct payment to the person or a third party to buy their own care.
- The person themselves directs the support that is available from the council.
- The council arranges the support.
- A mix of the above.

With self-directed support, the social care department first assesses the need for care, then does a financial assessment, and tells the person how much they need to contribute to their care and how much the social care department can do.

It's so complicated because basically you are working on two rules. You might also be trying to access continuing care which has an NHS source. What you get from the chancellor, what you get from the mayor and what you get from the health authority are different. It is shameful that the government is sitting on billions of unclaimed benefits because

*people don't claim. If we don't claim now, it might be withdrawn,
and people won't get it in the future. You are doing everyone a favour
if you claim now for yourself and the person you care for. (Carers'
organisation chief executive)*

All the addresses of the people who can help you navigate
through the maze are in Useful Contacts and Resources.

Three hints

1. No one can get their head round this unless it is their full-time
   job
2. There are organisations that can help
3. Not claiming helps no one, now or in the future

Sex and intimacy

Sex is intensely private and should be between consenting adults,
and in respect of older people it's a bit of a taboo. If it's with reference to our parents, we probably prefer not to know anything
about it. When you are a carer, you might also be the spouse or
partner of the person you care for. Particularly when carers from
outside the family are involved, it can become a difficult issue.
An example would be a care home that doesn't provide you with
privacy, or even a suitable bed for spouses or partners to make
love. That's very sad for both the carer and the person cared for.
A care home might even feel they are acting in the best interest
of your wife when they judge her incapable of consenting to sex,
and effectively prohibit you from intimacy.

Even a confused person can consent if they are able to understand information about sex, can remember this long enough to
help them decide about it on this occasion, use the information
to make a choice and remember it. No one should doubt that

this matter can be difficult and creates strong emotions in carers as well as care workers. One example of a condition that causes difficulty in relation to sex is frontal-lobe dementia. In these cases the person becomes disinhibited and less constrained by social norms. They might say and do things that are embarrassing or offensive and become sexually indiscriminate.

My brother and I disagreed about what to do when our mother started up a relationship with another resident in the care home. It seemed to David that she mistook him for our late father. I didn't mind but David was horrified. (Claire, sister of David, children of Rosie)

If Rosie has capacity, she is perfectly at liberty to make a relationship with whoever she wants. It doesn't matter how disconcerted David is. If the person you care for seems attracted sexually to another person in the care home, you may feel you have a right to put an end to it. Older people can be lonely and seek the comfort of human intimacy. All behaviour is communication. And Rosie is communicating that she wants a special friend. No one has an automatic right to stop that.

The guidance of the CQC (Care Quality Commission) is clear that even people with dementia can consent to sexual relations and care home staff must support that, unless there are signs of distress that might indicate there is a problem. It becomes more complicated when care staff from a wide range of social, ethnic, religious and educational backgrounds have varying views about whether older people should be interested in sex and allowed to express that interest. In the case of older homosexual men, the memory of legal and social discrimination may come rushing back because of negative attitudes of staff. Homes are trying to make sure that care workers understand that sex is not a problem to be managed but part of a resident's normal life. What the family carers think can be another issue.

The commonest sexual symptom of dementia is apathy and lack of interest. A relatively unusual symptom of dementia is hypersexuality, where the partner or spouse becomes aroused by very slight stimuli and makes sexual demands with a frequency and intensity which becomes intolerable or even abusive to the spouse/carer. If you are caring for someone with this symptom, you must seek help from your doctor.

Three hints

1. Sex is not a problem – it is part of normal life
2. You as a carer have a right to continue or discontinue an intimate relationship
3. The person you care for also has rights, but they are not limitless

Sleeplessness

Having a good sleep is vital for the person you are caring for. But you yourself will not be able to care if you're not given the chance to have a full night's sleep. We all know that sleep deprivation is used as a form of torture, and sometimes older people will torture us unintentionally. Older people need less sleep and people with dementia sleep even more lightly.

Exercise is a very good way of making someone tired and ensuring good, healthy sleep. Even if it is hard to get out and about, exercises in the chair can help. There are many YouTube videos if you search the internet under **'Chair exercises for seniors'**. This is where you must ask friends for help again because boredom, which leads to the person snoozing all day and being awake all night, can be relieved by having interesting things to do during the day. Friends may take the person out or keep them busy in the house for an hour or two.

Have a bedtime routine. It will be different for each person, but might involve a warm bath and winding down by putting off exciting television programmes and reducing the light level. If the person likes listening to the radio, press the snooze button so that it turns off after a while.

Research shows that people sleep better in a warm, comfortable bed in a cool room. Darkness is important for sleep. Even moonlight can be disturbing, so blackout blinds or curtains help. If a nightlight is needed to mark the path to the toilet in the night, you can find a movement sensor-activated light that will switch on when the person is getting out of bed.

Older people often have conditions that cause aches and pains for which they may be prescribed some pills. It is good to time that pain relief for bedtime so that the person isn't kept awake by their discomfort. If they are not sleeping, neither will you.

A doctor may offer a sedative to the person you care for if you are completely exhausted and the person is inclined to wake up agitated at night. This might help in the short term but can cause almost as many problems as it solves, because the person may not be completely awake in the day and snooze, so they are not tired when it is time to go to bed again. It might also make them unsteady on their feet.

Three hints

1. People want to sleep if they are tired
2. A bedtime routine, darkness and a cool room helps
3. Medication for pain may be more use than sedatives – ask the doctor

Social work assessment

When anyone comes to the house, Dad pulls himself together and brightens up, telling them he's fine. (Daughter)

Sometimes the person you care for lets the side down by being brilliant on the day of the assessment, giving the impression that no support is needed. When you have a social work assessment, it is hard to fall into the role of asking for help. You try to make the best of things most of the time, and when someone asks, you may not want to drone on about the worst things. In fact, you might not even remember them. Therefore you must write things down. The social worker doesn't need to know how things are when it is going fine. They want to know how bad it can get. They can't offer you help for things you don't mention, or they don't see, while assessing. This is important because that one assessment sets the ground for all the requests for help that you might make until the next assessment.

The questions were maddening. 'How often is your mother incontinent?' What does that even mean? She just IS incontinent! Do they want me to count up the pees and poos? If they mean how often do you have to change the bed, or wash sheets and clothes, and how long can she walk without wetting herself, why don't they ask that. But they just ask, 'How often is your mother incontinent?' (Retired nurse)

You can get help with the forms and the assessment from people with experience. Contact the local Age UK or carers' organisation. They sometimes have a member of staff who has a full-time job just supporting people to fill out forms. Because they do it every day it takes them a fraction of the time, and they can make sure that you don't miss out any relevant information that could increase the amount of benefit you get.

Three hints

1. You need to focus on the worst if you want support
2. The person you care for will subvert your attempt to get help
3. The questions are daft; get help with the forms from someone with experience

Spirituality

Religious observance is of crucial importance to many people but may become harder to continue in the circumstances that come with old age and being cared for. Having a religious belief is associated with lower stress levels. Engaging in familiar and safe practices like singing and attending worship can give comfort. How frailty is 'framed' or perceived in the mind of any human is shaped by their attitude to life, their personality, their belief in a soul, and so knowing how someone thinks about this is important for reducing stress. Some people might perceive dementia as a punishment from a deity for previous sins or wickedness, or as something to be accepted and borne on a journey to paradise. How people think of death and dying and how we respond to their spiritual needs makes a difference, even if that faith is different from our own. You might have to be like the Jewish lady singing Christian hymns to comfort a lady with dementia (https://www.youtube.com/watch?v=CCRDzRd8kgQ) or you could, in spite of being an atheist, find yourself reassuring someone that their God will not forget them. With dementia and caring for older people you have to do what works, even if you don't know why.

Malcolm Goldsmith, a priest with an interest in dementia, wrote *In a Strange Land*, still the finest book on dementia and religious faith. He examines questions from a Christian perspective.

People ask, 'Why me? Is this God's punishment?' They wrestle with ethical issues about the belief systems of those giving care. 'As a nurse can I pray with my patient?' Malcolm offers practical and supportive answers. Here I first read about the American nun Sister Laura. She feared she would forget Jesus because of dementia, and she said to the founding investigator of the Nun Study, David Snowdon, 'I finally realised that I may not remember Him, but He will remember me.'

All religions respect older people. The Qur'an recognises the effect of dementia in older people. It speaks of how some are 'sent back to a feeble age, so that they know nothing after having known much', and tells us that we must be kind to parents, and 'say not to them a word of contempt, nor repel them, but address them in terms of honour ... even as they cherished me in childhood.' Caring for ageing parents is incumbent on Muslims. The role of religion and people of faith in dementia care, and in supporting frail people to be well and contented, is very important.

Even people who have not been religious turn to faith during illness and at the end of life. They may start to think about the meaning of life, and struggle with coming to terms with ageing and change, with or without a concept of what God is to them. Health and social care worker training includes awareness of the spiritual needs of older people, but for you as a carer the need for awareness is different.

You can ask for help from your local faith leader or faith community. Many of the caring organisations that now identify as secular have their origins in faith communities. Although prayer and religious observance can take place anywhere, going to a church or other sacred space can be a peaceful and powerful experience. You can ask them to help you get the person to church if that is a practical problem. Religious observances provide an outlet for people who are lonely or worried. Live streaming of services offers a sense of community.

Being able to express comfort in spiritual terms is important for the sake of the person you care for, no matter what you yourself believe. It is ideal if you can also get comfort from shared beliefs. When an older person moves to a care setting such as a nursing home, ask the home and the church or faith group if they can support attendance at services or bring services into the care home. Volunteers from the faith group may offer companionship.

Five of our Filipina and Polish care assistants are very active in St Leonard's, the local Roman Catholic Church, and they work with their priest and the nuns to make sure that our older residents are included in worship any time they want. (Care home matron)

Three hints

1. Spirituality gets more important in times of trouble
2. Faith communities can and will help
3. Whether in a care setting or at home, faith community support is important

Stress

The first and most important thing about stress is to recognise it. It is when you're under pressure and feel unable to cope. It starts to affect the way you think, your sleep, your digestion – everything about your daily life. You get angry and impatient.

The second most important thing is to talk about it. It might feel bad to say out loud that caring for someone dependent on you is getting you down, but if your listener knows you and understands they will know that you are not a bad person.

Being a carer is a big job at the best of times even if things are going well, and sometimes they don't go well. In conversation with someone else you may discover sources of help that you didn't know about that will take some of the pressure off you. You may even find that just talking about it makes you feel better. Often people are stressed because they feel they should be doing more than they already are. Ideas in this book for reducing effort and increasing income might help.

Celebrate small victories when you make it through another day. Don't be too hard on yourself. Accept that you have done your best and no one can do any better than that. Focus on what you can control and don't worry about anything else. Take any help that will reduce your carer burden, but remember to be specific and ask people for the help you need. There is more advice on this in Chapter Five.

Three hints

1. Spot stress before it harms you
2. Talk to someone
3. Ask for help with your caring

Transport

Depending on where you live, you may be entitled to discounted travel on public transport when you accompany a person with disabilities. For example, if the person has a **Disabled Person's Railcard**, this qualifies you too for a discount when you travel with them by train. When you are looking for carers' travel and transport services, you can enter your postcode into the NHS online service search and find out what is available near you. This links you to a list of services which takes some time to search.

You might even find something you were not looking for. You may need a cup of tea for this job.

The rules about bus passes change from time to time and are different in each of the four parts of the UK, so check out the information on a website such as the **Carers Trust** (carers. org/public-transport/public-transport). The website gives a date when it was revised, and you might also find this information on the website of your local council. Many of the services depend on whether the person you care for is registered as disabled. This is another reason why getting a dementia diagnosis early is a good idea. In most places it will get you a Blue Badge.

Three hints

1. Take the benefit of concessions for your age group
2. Check with your local council for variations
3. Best current information will be on charity or local authority websites

Utilities

There are extra services available to help manage energy use if someone is on the **Priority Services Register**. The register is a free and voluntary system that your supplier uses to ensure the correct support is given to the most vulnerable customers. Those who qualify include people who have reached State Pension age, people who are disabled or have a long-term medical condition, and people who have a hearing or sight condition. If the older person you care for has dementia, that would count as a mental health condition for the purposes of the register.

You can apply by contacting the energy supplier or network operator. Give them your contact details and as much information as you can about the needs of the person you care for. The supplier passes the details to the network operator to add them to the register. If the person has a different supplier for gas and electricity you need to contact them both.

The help the vulnerable customer can get includes priority support in an emergency, so they could provide heating and cooking facilities if the supply is cut off. They can give advance notice of planned power cuts. If nobody can read the meter they can provide a meter-reading service or a smart meter. As a carer you can be nominated to receive communications and bills so that you can deal with them on behalf of the older person.

Some suppliers offer free gas safety checks every twelve months. You can request a safety check if the person lives alone or with others, has reached State Pension age and gets one of the means-tested benefits.

The Ofgem website at www.ofgem.gov.uk has details of social schemes such as the **Warm Home Discount**, which supports people who are living in fuel poverty or a fuel poverty-risk group. There is more about this in Chapter Three, as well as information about **Cold Weather Payments**. Suppliers are obliged to promote measures that improve the ability of low-income, fuel-poor and vulnerable households to heat their homes. The actions required are those that result in heat savings, such as the replacement of a broken heating system or the upgrade of an inefficient one. The larger suppliers can help if you are struggling with a bill. Ask them.

Three hints

1. Remember that keeping warm (or cool) is important
2. Check out whether you are eligible for any support schemes
3. The larger companies have trust funds if you are struggling to pay a debt

Wandering

Some writers about dementia are very emphatic that this is the wrong word for the behaviour when someone, confused and probably living with dementia, becomes lost. This is because it seems to them that 'wandering' is a word that suggests the person is moving aimlessly. In fact the person usually has an aim, but circumstances suggest that it is risky or inconvenient for everyone else because they lose their way or go out at a strange time in the wrong clothes. They might think they are going to work, to a job from which they retired decades ago. They might think they are going to the school gate to pick up their children, who are grown up and have children of their own. The person might be heading out in the snow in their shirtsleeves in the middle of the night, risking death from cold, but they might have a clear idea of what they want to do. They might be responding to an overwhelming need to get away from their current discomfort. The politically correct terms I see include 'walking about', 'unwanted exiting', 'elopement' and 'walking with purpose'. Families tend to call it wandering.

The worst nightmare is when the person you care for goes missing. Most carers call that wandering and will tell you about multiple incidents. The mixture of relief and anger when they return is sometimes channelled into trying to make their house as secure as a fortress to make sure that it doesn't happen again, which may only cause frustration and anger in the person who wants to walk about.

It can be useful to take a smartphone photo of the person each morning when they are dressed, in case later in the day you are asked to circulate a description of what they are wearing. There may be days when you can't even describe what you yourself are wearing, so it's no wonder you'd forget. People who go missing often go back to places they used to frequent, like a previous house, or back to the school to pick up the children, or back to work.

The section of this book on the **Herbert Protocol** describes a useful system that may exist in your area. It is based on some basic principles: the sooner you look for the person, the more people are looking and the more you know about their habits, the better your chance of finding them. Providing some biographical details, such as where the person usually likes to hang out (for example, their favourite café or shops), and a recent photograph allows the central control to send out an alert to many people to let them know that your person has gone missing. They suggest spending less than ten or fifteen minutes looking around the house and garden or street yourself before calling for help. You probably know that on average a missing adult usually turns up within twenty-four hours, and so the police are often reluctant to start a search within that time. If the person is registered on the protocol the police don't hesitate to start looking for them immediately.

The protocol would be less necessary if people carried locator devices. For example, family members can download an app on their smartphone which will allow them to locate each other on the phone's map within a few yards. That has the advantage that you can look at where they are and decide either not to worry or to go and retrieve them. It is sometimes called **geofencing**, because you can get an alert if the person goes beyond a boundary that you have agreed is safe. One problem is that the person you care for might go out without their phone. There are alternative **locator devices**, including those that look like a wristwatch or can be inserted into a shoe or other item of clothing. This makes them less likely to be left behind, but there are no guarantees. You will find more about this equipment on the AskSARA website, details in the Useful Contacts and Resources chapter and a link to the Herbert Protocol on your local authority website.

Three hints

1. Have an emergency plan after the first incident
2. Introduce a locator device early on
3. Join the Herbert Protocol

Young carers

If you are reading this as a young carer yourself, the strongest advice I can give you is this. Ask for help. The person you are caring for is not completely your responsibility. If they are an adult they have responsibility for themselves, and the health and social care system has responsibility for both of you. A teacher is a good person to talk to about problems because they can get you extra help with lessons. Your future depends on your education. Other young people at school or college may not understand the pressure that you are under, but good friends will appreciate what you are going through and talking with them often helps. The school might be able to give you support to keep in touch with the person you care for during the school day, for example letting you keep your phone on and allowing you to respond to calls. Most importantly, you need to ask the doctor, nurse or social worker whose job it is to help the person you are looking after to organise more formal support at home, to free you up to do your school, college or university work.

As with adult carers, you may not realise that you are a carer. It could be something that you started at a very young age, and you don't know any different. It could have happened overnight, for example if your parent had an accident or sudden illness and you had to take over their responsibilities, including caring for a grandparent. Even if you really want to help your family, you should not be working in the same way that adult carers do. You need to focus on school and further education and be free to do things that other people do at your age. It should be a matter of choice whether you do any caring. It is not just about whether you are willing. You may be the wrong person to be doing that caring. Because people with a disability or illness are entitled to support from health and social services, they should not have to rely on children.

Other school staff, such as counsellors or the school nurse, should be able to help. If you are missing lessons or not able to complete your homework and assignments they need to give you more support. School should be a place where you can just be like anyone else and forget about any problems at home. They can't understand if they don't know the pressure you are under. If you really don't want your school to know what is happening for you, you don't have to tell them. The problem then is that they can't make any adjustments for you. Is there one teacher that you feel you can confide in? It is always easier to talk about things if you make a list of what you want to say, and that could include a list of all the tasks you have to do. It would be good if someone in the family could write to the school on your behalf.

How other young people at school respond can be a problem. When people deliberately leave you out of activities or groups, that is bullying. Often we think of bullying as being called names, being physically attacked or threatened. But there are more subtle ways to make you feel bad about being different because of the caring pressures you are under. Of course, some people are bullied for no obvious reason, and most young people have been bullied at some point. However, you already have enough on your plate, so remember that there is support for you. It is totally understandable if you don't want to go to school because of bullying. Your feelings are valid. It's important to talk to an adult about it. There are organisations which have been set up for you to talk about the whole range of things you are dealing with. But getting an education is so important.

There is a section for young carers at the end of this book in Useful Contacts and Resources listing organisations that are there for young people and children. They may be able to tell you about local young carers' projects in your area. These can help you to meet up with other young carers. Apart from making new friends, it is a good way to have fun with people who have similar worries and challenges. You won't feel judged. Many of the projects can arrange for you to have a break from home and help you to relax. This may be at an evening club, days out and weekend or holiday breaks. They may also offer advice that will help you and your family.

Afterword

Writing this book has been an attempt to bring together as many useful and practical ideas as possible about things that could be helpful for people who are caring for an older relative, friend or neighbour. But it is also about telling the stories. Every carer is different, and every person being cared for is special, but years of talking with people and families have taught me that there are certain patterns which come up again and again as challenges in this situation. Research also uncovers these patterns, and that is why it is valuable to learn from the experience of others who may have found solutions, however imperfect, to the common problems. Carers sometimes feel as if they are invisible to society. We need to be visible to each other so that we can share ideas and information, and compare notes on what life is really like while caring for someone else and putting their needs before your own.

The people who speak through the pages of the book are anonymised. Never the less, many other people identify with them and even think I am writing about them in particular. They recognise, almost as stock characters, the eldest daughter who carries the main burden, the distant carer who worries about what is happening all the time even if they don't often visit, and other personalities featured in the stories. They laugh ruefully at the stories of older people who refuse the care that has been painstakingly put together, recognising that this often happens and has happened to them.

Because of the focus on problems and solutions, there has not been much space in this book to celebrate how astonishing carers are. I am in awe of their superpowers. They keep going when they are tired. They stay resilient when no one seems to hear their request for help. They bite their tongues when people swan into their lives distributing advice and swan out again without providing the help that the carer really needs, right at that moment.

Governments have repeatedly overlooked carers and their needs. As demand for care services has outstripped supply, particularly at times of crisis like the COVID-19 pandemic, family and friend carers have had to step in to bridge the gaps.

I wish I could change the attitude of the government, and that I could shake the magic money tree that would shower all carers with the things they need in order to do what they are selflessly doing. The least I can do is make this practical resource and send it out into the world with a message to all carers. What you are doing has been recognised through the ages as the basic condition of humanity, and what raises us up as being civilised. It has been required of us by religion and society. In this modern age the burden is greater than ever before because more of us live longer and with more ailments. But we still do it. And carers tell me about the joy and fulfilment that comes from caring.

One of the most important things that carers do for others is to make sure they know they are not alone. And I hope that as a carer, through the voices in this book, you will be aware that you are not alone either. We are all here to make each other feel safe.

Professor June Andrews

Useful Contacts and Resources

Here is an extensive list of resources, mainly linking to online references because the situation varies with every Budget and change of government, all mapped out for usefulness.

If you wish to contact me and find information on other books my website is www.juneandrews.net. You can also visit www.dementiatrust.org.uk for films about care homes, diagnosis and powers of attorney.

Books

June Andrews, *Dementia: The One-Stop Guide* (updated edition) (Souvenir Press, 2020)

June Andrews, *Care Homes: The One-Stop Guide* (Souvenir Press, 2020)

Sandra McDonald, *Power of Attorney: The One-Stop Guide* (Souvenir Press, 2021)

Official bodies

Care Inspectorate Wales

Registers, inspects and takes action to improve the quality and safety of services for the well-being of the people of Wales.

Welsh Government office

Sarn Mynach
Llandudno Junction
LL31 9RZ
0300 7900 126
Email: ciw@gov.wales
www.careinspectorate.wales

Department of Health and Social Care
Supports ministers in leading the nation's health and social care to help people live more independent, healthier lives for longer.
Ministerial Correspondence and Public Enquiries Unit
Department of Health and Social Care
39 Victoria Street
London SW1H 0EU
020 7210 4850 (weekdays from 9am to 5pm) and 0207 222 2262 (textphone) www.gov.uk/government/organisations/department-of-health-and-social-care

Department of Health Northern Ireland
Provides guidance on many issues of health and social care, policy and practice.
Department of Health
Castle Buildings
Stormont
Belfast BT4 3SQ
028 9052 0500
Email: webmaster@health-ni.gov.uk
www.health-ni.gov.uk

First-tier Tribunal (Care Standards) (England and Wales)
Responsible for handling appeals against decisions by the Care Quality Commission and others which exclude, remove or suspend someone

from a register to work with or care for children or vulnerable adults.
Care Standards Tribunal
HM Courts and Tribunals Service
1st Floor, Darlington Magistrates' Court
Parkgate DL1 1RU
01325 289 350
Email: cst@justice.gov.uk
www.gov.uk/courts-tribunals/first-tier-tribunal-care-standards

National Careers Service
Provides information on how to get back into the workplace — for people who have had a break in their careers.
https://nationalcareers.service.gov.uk/skills-assessment

NHS Direct
Information about health-related matters from the National Health Service.
www.nhs.uk

Northern Ireland nursing homes residents guide 2015
A link to the guide 'Minimum Standards for Nursing Homes set the criteria that providers have to meet in order to be registered with the Regulation and Quality Improvement Authority'.
www.health-ni.gov.uk/sites/default/files/publications/dhssps/care-standards-nursing-homes-residents-guide.pdf

Office of the Public Guardian, England and Wales
Helps people in England and Wales to stay in control of decisions about their health and finance and make important decisions for others who cannot decide for themselves.
PO Box 16185
Birmingham
B2 2WH

0300 456 0300

0115 934 2778 (textphone)

Email: customerservices@publicguardian.gov.uk

www.gov.uk/government/organisations/office-of-the-public-guardian

Office of the Public Guardian, Scotland

Maintains a public register of powers of attorney that have been registered, guardianship and intervention orders granted and authorisations granted under the access to funds scheme.

The Office of the Public Guardian

Hadrian House

Callendar Business Park

Callendar Road

Falkirk FK1 1XR

01324 678300

Email: OPG@scotcourts.gov.uk

www.publicguardian-scotland.gov.uk

Office of Care and Protection, Northern Ireland

The department of the court responsible for the administrative work associated with Part VIII of the Mental Health Order.

Room 2.2A, Second Floor

Royal Courts of Justice

Chichester Street

Belfast BT1 3JF

0300 200 7812

Email: OCP@courtsni.gov.uk

www.nidirect.gov.uk/contacts/contacts-az/office-care-and-protection

www.justice-ni.gov.uk/topics/courts-and-tribunals/office-care-and-protection-patients-section

Ombudsman Services
A free service that resolves disputes between consumers and companies that are signed up to their scheme.
3300 Daresbury Park
Warrington
Cheshire WA4 4HS
www.ombudsman-services.org

Financial Ombudsman Service
A free service that settles complaints between consumers and businesses that provide financial services.
0800 023 4567
Email: complaint.info@financial-ombudsman.org.uk
www.financial-ombudsman.org.uk

Citizen's advice on how to complain to an ombudsman:
https://www.citizensadvice.org.uk/consumer/get-more-help/how-to-use-an-ombudsman-in-england/

Parliamentary and Health Service Ombudsman
0345 015 4033
www.ombudsman.org.uk

Scottish Public Services Ombudsman
Bridgeside House
99 McDonald Road
Edinburgh EH7 4NS
0800 377 7330
www.spso.org.uk

Bereavement

AtaLoss.org
Provides information about how to access support for people who are bereaved in the UK.
PO Box 824
Chichester PO19 9WW
Email: office@ataloss.org
www.ataloss.org

Combat Stress
The UK's leading mental health charity for veterans offering free treatment and support to ex-servicemen and women of the UK Armed Forces.
0800 138 1619
07537 404 719 (Text)
Email: helpline@combatstress.org.uk
www.combatstress.org.uk

Cruse Bereavement Care
Provide help with understanding and coping with grief following the death of someone close.
0808 808 1677
Email: helpline@cruse.org.uk
www.cruse.org.uk

Department for Work and Pensions (DWP)
Contact the Bereavement Service to cancel the person's benefits and entitlements, including their State Pension. They'll also check if you're eligible for help with funeral costs or other benefits.
DWP Bereavement Service
0800 731 0469
0800 731 0464 (Textphone) (Monday to Friday, 9.30am–3.30pm)

Gov.uk – what to do when someone dies
https://www.gov.uk/browse/births-deaths-marriages/death
https://www.gov.uk/when-someone-dies

Humanist Ceremonies
A network of over 500 celebrants providing non-religious ceremonies and celebrants.
Humanists UK
39 Moreland Street
London EC1V 8BB
020 7324 3060
Email: ceremonies@humanism.org.uk
www.humanism.org.uk/ceremonies/non-religious-funerals

HM Revenue & Customs
For help with inheritance tax.
0300 123 1072 (general enquiries about inheritance tax)
www.gov.uk/inheritance-tax

Institute of Civil Funerals
A not-for-profit organisation that promotes the highest standards of funeral celebrancy for bereaved families and provides support and representation for its members.
Lytchett House
13 Freeland Park
Wareham Road
Poole
Dorset BH16 6FA
01480 861411
Email: admin@iocf.org.uk
www.iocf.org.uk

Marie Curie

UK leading end-of-life charity, providing nursing and hospice care, free support line available.

Support Line: 0800 090 2309

www.mariecurie.org.uk

National Bereavement Partnership

There is a support helpline for information, advice and support for people who are bereaved, plus counselling referral and befriending.

Helpline: 0800 448 0800 (7 a.m.–10 p.m. every day)

Email: helpline@nationalbereavementpartnership.org

www.nationalbereavementpartnership.org

National Records of Scotland

How to register a death.

0131 202 0451

www.nrscotland.gov.uk/registration/registering-a-death

The National Will Register

A place to search for registered wills.

Certainty, The National Will Register

The Mailbox

101 Wharfside Street

Birmingham

B1 1RF

0330 100 3660

Email: enquiries@certainty.co.uk

www.nationalwillregister.co.uk

NHS – on grief and how to get support via the NHS

https://www.nhs.uk/conditions/stress-anxiety-depression/coping-with-bereavement/

nidirect – who to tell about a death in NI
nidirect is the official government website for Northern Ireland citizens. The link below gives information about the process of reporting a death.
www.nidirect.gov.uk/articles/who-tell-about-death

Probate – how to apply
England and Wales: https://www.gov.uk/applying-for-probate
Scotland: https://www.scotcourts.gov.uk/taking-action/
dealing-with-a-deceased%27s-estate-in-scotland
Northern Ireland: https://www.nidirect.gov.uk/articles/
probate

Sue Ryder
Palliative, neurological and bereavement support.
www.sueryder.org/how-we-can-help/
online-bereavement-support

Tell Us Once
A service that lets you report a death to most government organisations in one go.
www.gov.uk/after-a-death/
organisations-you-need-to-contact-and-tell-us-once

Veterans' Gateway
Information, advice and support for any ex-service personnel and their families.
0808 802 1212
www.veteransgateway.org.uk

Veterans UK
If the person who died was receiving a war disablement pension, Veterans UK will help with the cost of a simple funeral.

0808 1914 2 18
Email: veterans-uk@mod.gov.uk
www.gov.uk/government/organisations/veterans-uk

Breaks and holidays

3H Fund

Provides subsidised group holidays in and around the UK for people with disabilities. You may also be able to apply for a grant to help towards the cost of a holiday.
3H Fund (Helping Hands for Holidays)
B2 Speldhurst Business Park
Langton Road,
Speldhurst, Tunbridge Wells,
Kent TN3 0AQ
01892 860 207
Email: info@3hfund.org.uk
www.3hfund.org.uk

AccessAble

An accessibility guide, providing information about the accessibility of various places.
AccessAble
18–20 High Street
Stevenage
Hertfordshire SG1 3EJ
01438 842 710
Email: hello@AccessAble.co.uk
www.accessable.co.uk

The Calvert Trust

Outdoor adventure activities in the countryside for disabled people, their families and friends – locations in Exmoor, Kielder and the Lake District.

The Lake District Calvert Trust
Little Crosthwaite, Keswick
Cumbria CA12 4QD
017687 72255
Email: enquiries@calvertlakes.org.uk
www.calvertlakes.org.uk

Calvert Kielder
Kielder Water & Forest Park
Hexham
Northumberland NE48 1BS
01434 250232
Email: enquiries@calvert-kielder.com
www.calvert-trust.org.uk

Calvert Trust Exmoor
Wistlandpound
Kentisbury, Barnstaple
Devon EX31 4SJ
01598 763 221
Email: exmoor@calvert-trust.org.uk
www.calvert-trust.org.uk

Caring Breaks (Northern Ireland only)

Graham House
Knockbracken Healthcare Park
Saintfield Road
Belfast BT8 8BH
028 9070 9118
www.caringbreaks.com

Disability Aid Trust

Pays towards the cost of a holiday care assistant for young people and adults with a physical disability (who are aged 17 and older) if they are unable to go on holiday without one.

PO Box 344
Lytham St Annes
Lancashire FY8 9JG
0800 028 0647
Email: secretary@disabilityaidtrust.org.uk
www.disabilityaidtrust.org.uk

Family Holiday Association

Provides breaks for UK families struggling with issues such as disability, severe and sudden illness, bereavement, mental health issues and domestic violence. Grants are given to low-income families who have not been on holiday for the past four years. The family must have at least one child under 18 years of age.

Family Holiday Association
7–14 Great Dover Street
London
SE1 4YR
020 3117 0650
Email: info@FamilyHolidayAssociation.org.uk
www.familyholidayassociation.org.uk

Holiday Homes Trust

A small charity which owns self-catering caravans which can cater for people with a disability or illness and low- or single-income families.

The Holiday Homes Trust
Gilwell Park
Chingford
London E4 7QW

020 8433 7290 and 020 8433 7291
Email: holiday.homes.trust@scouts.org.uk
www.holidayhomestrust.info

Options Holiday

Facilitates supported holidays for groups of adults with learning difficulties.
Options Supported Holidays Ltd.
Unit 4 Down Farm
South Cerney
Gloucestershire GL7 6DD
01285 740 491
Email: office@optionsholidays.co.uk
www.optionsholidays.co.uk

Shared Care Scotland (Scotland only)

They have an online directory of short break services and provide events, publications and research. They operate the Short Breaks Fund.
Unit 2, Dunfermline Business Centre
Izatt Avenue
Dunfermline
Fife KY11 3BZ
01383 622462
Email: office@sharedcarescotland.com
www.sharedcarescotland.org.uk

Traveleyes

A service which provides independent group holidays for people who are blind, partially sighted and fully sighted.
PO Box 511
Leeds 3JT
0113 834 6094
www.traveleyes-international.com

Information about caring

Advice NI

Exists to provide leadership and services to its sixty-nine member organisations and to ensure accessible advice services across Northern Ireland. Delivers a range of advice services to the public including benefits, personal and business debt, EU Settlement Scheme, tax credits and other HMRC services.

Forestview
Purdy's Lane
Newtownbreda
Belfast BT8 7AR
0800 915 4604
Email: advice@adviceni.net
www.adviceni.net

Bathing without a Battle

Descriptions and tips for different bathing techniques, such as the towel bath, recliner bath, toilet or commode bath and others. A training dvd is available as well as a list of useful products and supplies.

Email: info@bathingwithoutabattle.unc.edu
www.bathingwithoutabattle.unc.edu/bathing-techniques

Care Choices

Information about how to find a care home or alternative care solution.

www.carechoices.co.uk

Care England

Representative body for small, medium and large providers in England.

2nd Floor, 40 Artillery Lane

London EI 7LS
08450 577 677
020 7492 4840
Email: info@careengland.org.uk
www.careengland.org.uk

Care Quality Commission in England (CQC)
An independent regulator of health and social care in England.
03000 616161
Email: enquiries@cqc.org.uk
www.cqc.org.uk

Care Inspectorate in Scotland
Looks at the quality of care in Scotland to ensure it meets high standards. If they find that improvement is needed, they support services to make positive changes.
Compass House
11 Riverside Drive
Dundee DDI 4NY
0345 600 9527
Email: enquiries@careinspectorate.gov.scot
www.careinspectorate.com

Carers Direct
Provides a home caring service for elderly and less able people living in their own homes in the west of Scotland.
31 James Street
Helensburgh G84 8AS
01436 671389
www.carersdirect.com

Carers Trust

Raises awareness and supports unpaid carers in the UK
www.carers.org

Carers Trust
Unit 101, 164–180 Union Street
London SE1 0LH
0300 772 9600
Email: info@carers.org

Carers Trust Wales
Transport House
1 Cathedral Road
Cardiff CF11 9HA
0300 772 9702 (Wales)
Email: wales@carers.org

Carers Trust Scotland (including Young Carers)

The largest provider of comprehensive carer support services in Scotland.
Carers Trust Scotland
Spaces, Tay House
300 Bath Street
Glasgow G2 4JR
0300 772 7701
Email: scotland@carers.org
www.carers.org/our-work-in-scotland
www.carers.org/young-carer-and-young-adult-carer-work-in-scotland

Carers UK

Provides advice, information and support to carers and about caring, connects carers with others and with support, campaigns and improves services for carers.

0808 808 7777
Email: advice@carersuk.org
www.carersuk.org
Carers Scotland: www.carersuk.org/scotland
Carers NI: www.carersuk.org/northernireland
Carers Wales: www.carersuk.org/wales
Local support: www.carersuk.org/help-and-advice/
get-support/local-support

Citizens Advice

A national charity and network of local charities offer confidential advice online, over the phone, and in person, for free.
www.citizensadvice.org.uk
Citizens Advice Scotland: www.citizensadvice.org.uk/
scotland/
Citizens Advice NI: www.citizensadvice.org.uk/about-us/
northern-ireland/
Citizens Advice Wales: www.citizensadvice.org.uk/wales/

Coalition of Carers in Scotland

Exists to advance the voice of carers by facilitating carer engagement and bringing carers and local carer organisations together with decision makers at a national and local level.
PO Box 21624
Stirling FK7 1EF
01786 850247
Email: coalition@carersnet.org
www.carersnet.org

Disability Information Scotland

Provides information for people living with disability in Scotland.
168 Bath Street
Glasgow G2 4TP

0300 323 9961 (Helpline)
0778 620 0707 (Text)
Email: info@disabilityscot.org.uk
www.disabilityscot.org.uk

FirstStop Care Advice

Offers independent, impartial and free advice about housing and care options for later life.
Suite A, 202 Lambeth Road
London SE1 7JW
0800 377 7070 (for older people)
Email: info@firststopadvice.org.uk
www.firststopcareadvice.org.uk

Independent Age

Offers regular contact and campaigning, plus free impartial advice about care and support, money and benefits, and health and mobility.
18 Avonmore Road
London W14 8RR
0800 319 6789
Email: charity@independentage.org
www.independentage.org

MECOPP Carers Service
The Minority Ethnic Carers of People Project

Offers support for Black and minority ethnic carers at a national level.
Maritime House
8 The Shore
Edinburgh EH6 6QN
Main line: 0131 467 2994
Chinese language line: 0131 467 2996
Asian language line: 0131 467 2997
Email: info@mecopp.org.uk

www.mecopp.org.uk

Northern Ireland Regulation and Quality Improvement Authority (RQIA)

The independent body responsible for monitoring and inspecting the availability and quality of health and social care services in Northern Ireland, and encouraging improvements in the quality of those services.

028 9536 IIII
Email: info@rqia.org.uk
www.rqia.org.uk

Relatives and Residents Association

National charity for older people in or needing care and the relatives and friends who help.

020 7359 8136 (9.30am–1pm Monday to Friday, 6–8pm Thursdays)
Email: helpline@relres.org
www.relres.org

Shared Lives Plus

Care and support service.

G04 The Cotton Exchange
Old Hall Street
Liverpool L3 9JR
01512273499
Email: info@sharedlivesplus.org.uk
www.sharedlivesplus.org.uk

Shelter England

Supporting anybody struggling with bad housing or homelessness, or anything related in England.

Urgent advice line: 0808 800 4444

https://england.shelter.org.uk
Find local services: https://england.shelter.org.uk/get_help/local_services

Shelter Scotland
Supporting anybody struggling with bad housing or homelessness, or anything related in Scotland.
4th floor, Scotiabank House
6 South Charlotte Street
Edinburgh EH2 4AW
0808 800 4444
Email: info@shelter.org.uk
https://scotland.shelter.org.uk

Solicitors for the Elderly
Specialist group of lawyers to support older and vulnerable people.
Sue Carraturo, Administrator
SFE, PO Box 541
Hoddesdon EN11 1SE
0844 567 6173
www.sfe.legal

SOLLA (Society of Later Life Advisers)
Advice about a financial assessment or financing a care home.
0333 2020 454
Email: admin@societyoflaterlifeadvisers.co.uk
www.societyoflaterlifeadvisers.co.uk

United Kingdom Homecare Association (UKHCA)
Professional association of home care providers in all sectors.
UKHCA
Sutton Business Centre
Restmor Way

Wallington
Surrey SM6 7AH
020 8661 8188
Email: enquiries@ukhca.co.uk
www.ukhca.co.uk

Which? Later life Care information pages
www.which.co.uk/later-life-care

Charities for specific conditions

Alzheimer's Society
Information on legal and welfare issues.
Scott Lodge
Scott Road
Plymouth PL2 3DU
Dementia Connect Support Line: 0333 150 3456 (in English)
03300 947 400 (in Welsh)
www.alzheimers.org.uk

Diabetes UK
Provides information about diabetes.
Wells Lawrence House
126 Back Church Lane
London E1 1FH
0345 123 2399
email:helpline@diabetes.org.uk
www.diabetes.org.uk

Disability Rights UK
Campaigns for the rights of people with disabilities.
Plexal
14 East Bay Lane

Here East
Queen Elizabeth Olympic Park
Stratford
London E20 3BS
0330 995 0400
Email: enquiries@disabilityrightsuk.org
www.disabilityrightsuk.org

Living Made Easy (formerly Disabled Living Foundation)
Provision of free and impartial advice for people with disabilities.
0300 999 0004
Email: info@dlf.org.uk
www.livingmadeeasy.org.uk

Macmillan Cancer Support
Emotional, physical and financial support for those with cancer.
0808 808 00 00
https://www.macmillan.org.uk

Mencap
Support for people with a learning disability.
Helpline: 0808 808 1111 (England and Northern Ireland)
0808 8000 300 (in Wales)
Email: helpline@mencap.org.uk
www.mencap.org.uk

Phab England
Aims to inspire and support disabled and non-disabled people to get along together.
Summit House
50 Wandle Road
Croydon
Surrey CR0 1DF
020 8667 9443

Email: info@phab.org.uk
www.phab.org.uk

Stroke Association
Supporting people after a stroke.
0303 3033 100
Email: helpline@stroke.org.uk
www.stroke.org.uk

Child and young carers

Action for Children
Can put you in touch with other young carers and offers free places for young carers at its residential activity camps.
Children's Services Support Centre (Head office)
3 The Boulevard
Ascot Road
Watford WD18 8AG
0300 123 2112
Email: ask.us@actionforchildren.org.uk
www.actionforchildren.org.uk/our-work-and-impact/
children-and-families/young-carers/

Action for Children, NI Regional Young Carers
02890 460500
Email: niyoungcarers@actionforchildren.org.uk
www.actionforchildren.org.uk/how-we-can-help/our-local-
services/find-our-services-near-you/ni-regional-young-carers/

Childline
You can talk to someone who may be able to give you advice and get you help. They will not tell anyone that you have called. It is a free and confidential helpline.

0800 11 11
www.childline.org.uk

The Children's Society
Can help you understand your rights as a young carer, introduce you to other young carers, advise you on different ways into education and employment. They run the Young Carers Festival and fund projects for young carers.
The Children's Society
Whitecross Studios
50 Banner Street
London EC1Y 8ST
0300 303 7000
Email: supportercare@childrenssociety.org.uk
www.childrenssociety.org.uk

Edinburgh Young Carers
Helping young carers in Edinburgh.
Edinburgh Young Carers
Norton Park
57 Albion Road
Edinburgh EH7 5QY
0131 475 2322
Email: info@youngcarers.org.uk
www.youngcarers.org.uk

KIDS
An organisation specially for carers under the age of 18. It runs regular clubs where you can meet other young carers and offers support, advice and information.
7–9 Elliott's Place
London N1 8HX
0207 359 3635
www.kids.org.uk/young-carers

NHS – page on young carers

How to access help and information.
www.nhs.uk/conditions/social-care-and-support-guide/
support-and-benefits-for-carers/being-a-young-carer-your-
rights/

Social worker

You or your parents can request a visit from a social worker from the local council.
Social Work England: www.socialworkengland.org.uk
Social Work Scotland: www.socialworkscotland.org
Social Care Council (NI): www.niscc.info
Social Care Wales: www.socialcare.wales

Young Minds – help for Young Carers

https://youngminds.org.uk/find-help/looking-after-yourself/
young-carers/

Young Scot – help for Young Carers

Information about how to apply for funding and other forms of help for young carers in Scotland.
www.young.scot/campaigns/national/young-carers

Child and young carers – legal information
Coram Children's Legal Centre

Legal advice for England and Wales.
Wellington House, 4th Floor
90–92 Butt Road
Colchester
Essex CO3 3DA
www.childrenslegalcentre.com

Child Law Advice

Legal advice for England and Wales.
Family or child law: 0300 330 5480
Education law: 0300 330 5485
www.childlawadvice.org.uk

Children's Law Centre NI

Advice and information on young people's rights in Northern Ireland.
Children's Law Centre, Rights House
127–131 Ormeau Road
Belfast BT7 1SH
(028) 9024 5704
0808 808 5678 (Freephone advice line)
Email: chalky@childrenslawcentre.org
www.childrenslawcentre.org.uk

Scottish Child Law Centre

*Free legal advice service is provided via telephone and email on all
aspects of Scots law relating to children and young people, including
education; additional support needs; health; confidentiality; social
work; residence; contact; children's rights; youth offending; and access
to records. Advice given by qualified solicitors.*
For under 21s: 0800 328 8970 (from landline), 0300 3301421 (from
mobile)
For parents, carers and professionals: 0131 667 6333
Email: advice@sclc.org.uk
www.sclc.org.uk

Funding

Attendance Allowance

Helps with extra costs if you have a disability severe enough for you to

need someone to help look after you.
0800 731 0122
0800 731 0317 (Textphone, Mon to Fri 8am to 6pm)
Relay UK (if you cannot hear or speak on the phone): 18001
then 0800 731 0122
Video relay service for British Sign Language (BSL) users –
check you can use this service
www.gov.uk/attendance-allowance

Carer's Allowance Unit (England, Wales, Scotland)
Get information about how to make a Carer's Allowance claim.
0800 731 0297
0800 731 0317 (Textphone)
www.gov.uk/carers-allowance-unit

Centre for Independent Living NI (Northern Ireland only)
Provides information and advice on getting direct payments, using personal budgets and employing carers and personal assistants.
Linden House
Beechill Business Park
96 Beechill Road
Belfast BT8 7QN
028 9064 8546
Email: info@cilni.org
www.cilni.org

Disability and Carers Service (NI)
Administers Disability Living Allowance, Attendance Allowance, Carer's Allowance and Carer's Credit.
Disability Living Allowance OR Attendance Allowance OR
Carer's Allowance
Disability & Carers Service
Mail Opening Unit

PO Box 42
Limavady BT49 4AN
0800 587 0912
0800 012 1574 (Textphone)
Email: dcs.incomingpostteamdhc2@dfcni.gov.uk
www.nidirect.gov.uk/contacts/disability-and-carers-service

Family Fund
Provides grants towards major costs for a wide range of items and other services for families on a low income who are caring for a child with a severe disability.
4 Alpha Court
Monks Cross Drive
York YO32 9WN
01904 550 055
Email: info@familyfund.org.uk
www.familyfund.org.uk

Money Helper
Brings together the support and services of three government-backed financial guidance providers: the Money Advice Service, the Pensions Advisory Service and Pension Wise.
Money and Pensions Service
120 Holborn
London ECIN 2TD
0800 138 7777 (Pensions guidance for all ages)
+44 20 3553 2279 (From overseas)
www.moneyhelper.org.uk/en

Turn2us
Has a benefits calculator and can provide practical support to those struggling financially, a national charity which can also provide its own grants.

0808 802 2000

www.turn2us.org.uk

Hospices

Hospice UK

Provides information about hospices and hospice care, including a hospice finder that connects you to local hospices UK wide for short or long stays.

Hospice UK

34–44 Britannia Street

London WC1X 9JG

020 7520 8200

Email: info@hospiceuk.org

www.hospiceuk.org

Macmillan Cancer Support

A charity offering emotional, physical and financial support for those with cancer, including advice on end-of-life care.

0808 808 00 00 (Support line)

www.macmiilan.org.uk

Marie Curie

The UK leading end-of-life charity, providing nursing and hospice care – locations across the country.

0800 716 146 (General queries)

0800 090 2309 (Free Helpline)

www.mariecurie.org.uk

Mental health and relationship support

Mind

Charity to support people with their mental health problems, including help with bereavement.

15–19 Broadway
Stratford
London E15 4BQ
Infoline: 0300 123 3393
Email: info@mind.org.uk
www.mind.org.uk

Relate

The UK's largest provider of relationship support.
0300 0030396
www.relate.org.uk

Rethink Mental Illness

Works to improve the lives of people severely affected by mental illness through a network of groups and services, information and campaigning.
Advice line: 0808 801 0525
www.rethink.org

Samaritans

Offers listening and support to anyone in need.
Freepost SAMARITANS LETTERS
Free phoneline: 116 123 (Any time, day or night)
Email: jo@samaritans.org
www.samaritans.org

Older people

Age UK

Advice and information for people in later life through Age UK advice line, publications and online.

Tavis House
1–6 Tavistock Square
London WC1H 9NA
0800 678 1602
www.ageuk.org.uk

Age Cymru

Vital services for older people in the community in Wales.

Ground Floor
Mariners House
Trident Court
East Moors Road
Cardiff CF24 5TD
0800 022 3444, 0300 303 44 98
Email: advice@agecymru.org.uk
www.agecymru.org.uk

Age NI

Advice and support for older people in Northern Ireland.

3 Lower Crescent
Belfast BT7 1NR
0808 808 7575
www.ageni.org

Age Scotland

Advice and support for older people in Scotland.

Causewayside House
160 Causewayside

Edinburgh EH9 1PR

t: 0800 124 4222

www.agescotland.org.uk

Associated Retirement Community Operators (ARCO)

The main body representing the Retirement Community sector in the UK.

Associated Retirement Community Operators

The Heals Building, Suites A&B, 3rd Floor

22–24 Torrington Place

London WC1E 7HJ

0203 697 1204

www.arcouk.org

Association of Retirement Housing Managers (ARHM)

Promotes high standards of ethics and practice in the management of retirement housing.

ARHM

1–3 Manor Road

Chatham ME4 6AE

t: 0797 431 1421

Email: enquiries@arhm.org

www.arhm.org

Hourglass (formerly Action Against Elder Abuse)

A charity working to end the harm and abuse of older people in the UK, with a free helpline for those suffering from abuse.

0808 808 8141 (Helpline)

Email: enquiries@wearehourglass.org (England)

cymru@wearehourglass.org (Wales)

scotland@wearehourglass.org (Scotland)

nireland@wearehourglass.org (N Ireland)

www.wearehourglass.org

Respite

After Umbrage

A charity that provides free short breaks for anyone who has been looking after family members or loved ones with life-limiting or terminal conditions.

www.afterumbrage.org.uk

Hospice UK

Provides information about hospices and has a list of local hospices UK-wide for shorter or longer stays.

Hospice UK
34–44 Britannia Street
London WC1X 9JG
020 7520 8200
Email: info@hospiceuk.org
www.hospiceuk.org

Leonard Cheshire

Provides a range of practical support services for people with disabilities and their families and carers.

020 3242 0200 (England)
0131 346 9040 (Scotland)
01633 422 583 (Wales)
028 9024 6247 (Northern Ireland)
Email: info@leonardcheshire.org, scotlandoffice@leonardcheshire.org, walesoffice@leonardcheshire.org, northernirelandoffice@leonardcheshire.org
www.leonardcheshire.org

The Ogilvie Charities

Offer sheltered accommodation in Suffolk and Essex and also make grants to support respite holidays for carers.

The Gate House
9 Burkitt Road
Woodbridge
Suffolk IP12 4JJ
01394 388746
Email: ogilviecharities@btconnect.com
www.ogilviecharities.org.uk/funding-for-holidays-for-carers

Revitalise

A charity providing respite care in a holiday setting for disabled people and carers for over fifty years. Funding may be available for holidays.
0303 303 0145
Email: bookings@revitalise.org.uk
www.revitalise.org.uk

Shared Care Scotland

Provides information about short breaks for carers, including a short breaks directory.
Unit 2, Dunfermline Business Centre
Izatt Avenue
Dunfermline
Fife KY11 3BZ
01383 622462
Email: office@sharedcarescotland.com
www.sharedcarescotland.org.uk

Acknowledgements

I would like to thank Cindy Chan, Graeme Hall, Linden Lawson and all the staff at Souvenir Press and Profile Books for their help and encouragement. Also, Andrew Franklin for starting me on this journey, and his unfailing enthusiasm along the way.

Without the Dementia Services Development Trust (www. dementiatrust.org.uk) I would not be able to undertake this work, and I'm particularly grateful to the Chair Sandra McDonald and the Rev Nigel Robb for their advice and support.

I am grateful to all the families and carers who have shared their views with me, and the older people receiving care who have spoken to me about the experience. Their anonymised and edited words have been used to illustrate common themes.

My sister Hazel McKay spent a long time reading the manuscript and spotted typos that I had completely missed. I am grateful to her for that patience and care.

Finally, I thank Sonia Mangan, who read every chapter as I went along, keeping me appraised of the real lives of the carers she works with every day. We have known each other since we were ward sisters in London hospitals at the end of the last century. It sounds like a long time ago, but it feels like yesterday.

Index